Charles John Cornish

Animals of To-Day

Their life and conversation

Charles John Cornish

Animals of To-Day
Their life and conversation

ISBN/EAN: 9783337095031

Printed in Europe, USA, Canada, Australia, Japan

Cover: Foto ©Andreas Hilbeck / pixelio.de

More available books at **www.hansebooks.com**

ANIMALS OF TO-DAY

A BRITISH BEAVER.

ANIMALS OF TO-DAY
THEIR LIFE AND
CONVERSATION

BY

C. J. CORNISH

Author of 'Life at the Zoo,' 'Wild England'
'Animals at Work and Play,' etc.

WITH SIXTEEN ILLUSTRATIONS

LONDON
SEELEY AND CO. LIMITED
38 GREAT RUSSELL STREET
1898

PREFACE

THE following chapters were originally contributed to the *Spectator*, to the editor of which I have to offer my thanks for permission to publish them in a collected form.

I am also much indebted to Mr. Charles Reid, of Wishaw, our leading photographic artist in the domain of outdoor natural history, for the choice of many of the illustrations from his large collection.

C. J. CORNISH.

CONTENTS

		PAGE
I.	REINDEER AND SNOW-CAMELS	1
II.	GOATS IN CITIES	9
III.	THE 'NEW' PIG	17
IV.	THE STORY OF THE JERSEY HERD	25
V.	THE CAT ABOUT TOWN	33
VI.	A 'WOULD-BE' HELPER: THE FRIENDLY PUMA	41
VII	ANIMAL COLONISTS	49
VIII.	IRISH DONKEYS FOR SOUTH AFRICA	57
IX.	SHIRE HORSES AT ISLINGTON	64
X.	THE BEAUTY OF CATTLE	72
XI.	WAR-HORSES	80
XII.	THE SPEED OF THE PIGEON-POST	87
XIII.	THE LONDON HORSE AT HOME	94
XIV.	MENAGERIE ANIMALS	102
XV.	ANIMALS IN FAMINE	109
XVI.	PLAGUE-STRUCK ANIMALS	117
XVII.	THE ANIMAL 'CHAPTER OF ACCIDENTS'	124
XVIII.	THIRSTY ANIMALS	131
XIX.	THE EFFECT OF HEAT ON ANIMALS	138
XX.	ANIMALS IN THE DARK	145
XXI.	NATURAL DEATH IN THE ANIMAL WORLD	152

		PAGE
XXII.	ANIMALS' ILLUSIONS	160
XXIII.	ANIMAL ANTIPATHIES	166
XXIV.	ANIMAL KINDERGARTEN	174
XXV.	THE RANGE OF ANIMAL DIET	181
XXVI.	DAINTIES OF ANIMAL DIET	188
XXVII.	THE SLEEPING HOMES OF ANIMALS	195
XXVIII.	THE CARRIAGE OF ANIMALS	203
XXIX.	TRESPASSING ANIMALS	212
XXX.	DO ANIMALS TALK?	219
XXXI.	ANIMALS UNDERGROUND	227
XXXII.	MAMMALS IN THE WATER	235
XXXIII.	CROCODILES	243
XXXIV.	MARSUPIALS AND THEIR SKINS	251
XXXV.	WILD BEASTS' SKINS IN COMMERCE	258
XXXVI.	EAGLES ON AN ENGLISH LAKE	266
XXXVII.	THE GREAT FOREST EAGLE	273
XXXVIII.	THE PAST AND FUTURE OF BRITISH MAMMALS	280
XXXIX.	THE RETURN OF THE GREAT BUSTARD	288
XL.	BIG GAME	296
XLI.	GAME PRESERVATION IN THE UNITED STATES	304
XLII.	ANIMAL ACCLIMATIZATION AT WOBURN ABBEY	312

LIST OF ILLUSTRATIONS

	PAGE
A BRITISH BEAVER	*Frontispiece*
GOATS IN A TIMBER-YARD	12
THE CAT AS WILD ANIMAL	36
UNWELCOME COLONISTS	50
ROB ROY'S CATTLE	74
HARD TIMES ON EXMOOR	110
BEAVER IN THE WATER	114
COOL QUARTERS—HIGHLAND CATTLE	142
KITTEN'S KINDERGARTEN	174
A FIRST-CLASS CARRIAGE, BOSTOCK'S MENAGERIE	206
A TRESPASSING PARTY	216
LEAVING THE EARTH	228
AN ANCIENT BRITON	232
OTTER SWIMMING A STREAM	236
OTTER ON A LAKE SIDE	284
AN ENGLISH-BRED GAZELLE	314

INTRODUCTION

THIRTY years ago it seemed possible that the main range of animal usefulness, except as supplying food, might be covered by mechanical contrivance, guided by human intelligence.

So much had been achieved by inventors that the old-fashioned animal 'helpers and servers' were at a discount, and there was a general disregard of animal life, and a waste of it, both directly and indirectly.

In the last few years a reaction of feeling has taken place, both in this country and its colonies, and in the United States. The animal factor is no longer at a discount. Some of the most practical persons in the world believe, apart from any promptings of sentiment, that it pays to make the best use of the 'machines' patented by Nature, and the service of animals is taking a higher place in many of the intelligent combinations of modern life. Not only are highly-specialized animals, like the reindeer, the snow-camel, and others, in request for modern enterprise: the more delicate animal 'machines' guided by organs of sense and perception superior to ours are employed on a great and increasing scale for naval and military purposes—dogs, for instance, as watchers and messengers in the French, German, and Italian armies, and the pigeon-post by all the Western Powers. Recent experiments even indicate that the bloodhound will be once more used for police purposes.

How some of the wild animals have managed to maintain themselves during the bad times of the nineteenth century, their shifts and expedients, and personal idiosyncrasies, and instances of their survival under difficulties, are set out in many of the following chapters. Others deal with the wonderful progress of the domesticated kinds, such as the Jersey cattle, the shire horse, pig, the goat in cities, and other breeds whose adaptation to the needs or conditions of this century has been rapid and astonishing.

I.—REINDEER AND SNOW-CAMELS

THE place still held by animals in the practical life of to-day is well shown by the efforts of the Governments of Canada and the United States to supply transport to Klondike during the spring of 1898. To reach an ice-beleaguered goldfield in the north-western corner of Arctic America, the Governments of two great nations, Canada and the United States, were sending agents to fetch half-wild reindeer, and Lapps, their half-wild owners, from the north-eastern corner of Arctic Europe. This astonishing adventure was undertaken, first, because the reindeer are the only draught animals which can find food on the journey to Klondike, and secondly, because in the race against time there was not an hour to spare in organizing untrained herds. Broken reindeer, with their own Lapp owners and drivers, had to be procured, or the expedition would have been too late to start from Dyea in March, when the Arctic days are lengthening. Meantime, the Canadian Government, at its wits' end to supply its own police-force on the way to Klondike, also sent an agent to Norway, who forwarded six Lapps and a hundred and fourteen deer, and was instructed to send an equal number as soon as he could get them.

Everyone knows that all this trouble, expense and hurry to obtain some two thousand five hundred medium-sized deer from the uttermost parts of the earth is due solely to one physical fact in natural history—namely, that these deer can find food where no other beast of burden can. But the exact physical and local conditions which should make it possible for the deer to cross where two thousand horses were already lying dead from starvation are the following. The road lies mainly beyond the northern limit of grass and trees. The reindeer will eat moss, and prefers it to other food. Moss, as we understand it, is rather an uncommon vegetable. It would be difficult, for instance, to find enough moss by an English roadside to feed one reindeer per diem, not to speak of hundreds. But once beyond a certain line on the Arctic fringe, moss is the one common form of vegetable life. Lichen is the more appropriate name, for it is a thick, whitish growth, springing up naturally, and often burnt by the Lapps over large tracts to produce a thicker crop for the deer, just as Scotch shepherds burn the heather. It is the natural vegetable covering of the earth, where earth, and not rock, is on the surface. And the Klondike climate is particularly favourable to this moss, which lies over the whole soil, an invisible vegetable lining, between the earth and the covering snow. It is so thick that even in summer, when the snow melts, this non-conducting layer of moss prevents the ground from thawing. Before the snow melts, the deer would be travelling over one vast carpet of snow-covered food; and as each reindeer, male or female, has a projecting palmated antler, or 'snow-scraper,' with a few sidelong sweeps of which it can brush away the snow, the herds have no trouble in reaching their food.

When communications with Klondike were once more open, it was found that the miners were not in such straits as was supposed. But the story is evidence that the animal factor is not yet struck out of the lists of human needs.

When the purchase of these reindeer was announced, I received from Mr. Carl Hagenbeck, of Hamburg, a suggestion of another transport animal for use in the snows of Klondike. 'The best animal for the Klondike climate,' he wrote, 'is the big Siberian camel. These camels transport all merchandise from China to Russia, and can stand Siberian cold as well as the greatest heat. They never need shelter, and sleep out in the deep snow. . . . They can carry from five hundredweight to six hundredweight, and also go in harness and pull as much as a big horse. They can cross mountains as well as level country. As for the difficulty of procuring them, there is none. I can deliver as many as may be wanted for forty pounds apiece in London or Grimsby, or sixty pounds, duty paid, in New York.' The two-humped Bactrian camel, of which Mr. Hagenbeck speaks, is the only beast of burden, not excepting the reindeer, of which Englishmen have absolutely no practical experience. The Russians are, in fact, the only Europeans who are acquainted with this universal beast of transport of Northern Asia, while in Europe itself it has not been seen since the revolt of the Tartars in the reign of the Empress Catharine.

In that memorable and blood-stained exodus, when the Tartars fled from the banks of the Volga to the Great Wall of China, their herds of snow-camels alone saved the remnant of the people; and when, after five months, the flying horde, reduced from six hundred thousand to three hundred and fifty thousand souls, together with the pursuing Bashkirs, plunged into the waters of the Lake of Tengis, 'like a host of lunatics pursued by a host of fiends,' they were still riding on the camels on which they had started in the snows of winter, and crossed the ice of the Russian rivers. 'Ox, cow, horse, mule, ass, sheep, or goat, not one survived,' writes De Quincey, 'only the camels. These arid and adust creatures, looking like the mummies of some antediluvian animals, without the affections or sensibilities of flesh and blood—these only lifted their speaking eyes to the Eastern heavens, and had to all appearance come out of this long tempest of trial unscathed and hardly diminished.' These 'innumerable camels' were all of the Bactrian breed, and evidence of the extremes of cold and heat endured in this enterprise of the Kalmucks may be found in the fact that, during the early stages of the flight, circles of men, women and children were found frozen stiff round the camp-fires in the morning, while in the last stage the horde passed for ten days through a waterless desert with only an eight-days' supply, and yet arrived 'without sensible loss' of these creatures on the shore of the Chinese lake.

The constant references to the Bactrian camels made by De Quincey, and his careful repetition of their distinctive name, show his appreciation of the part they played. But in the end he is still under the dominion of the accepted opinion about camels in general. They are 'arid and adust'—creatures of the sand and the hot desert, rather than of the mountain and the cold desert or steppe, and the South Siberian snows. It is this distinction of habit and habitat which gives novelty to Mr. Hagenbeck's suggestion. The physical barrier of the Himalayas and the Hindoo-Khoosh not only separates the two species with a completeness not seen in the case of any other breed of domesticated animal, but has relegated one solely to the use of the yellow men, and the other to the service of the black or brown men. The camel of the North, which can endure not only thirst, but freezing cold, long spells of hunger, and a bed of snow, is not only the stronger, but the better equipped species. Before the summer heat it sheds its coat; but by September it grows a garment of fur almost as thick as a buffalo robe, and equally cold-resisting. It is far more strongly built than the Southern camel. It does not 'split' when on slippery ground, though it falls on moist, wet clay, which yields to the foot. On ice and frozen snow it stands firmly, and can travel far, partly because it has developed a harder foot-pad than the Southern species, partly because it has a kind of claw-toe projecting beyond the pad of the foot. Major Leonard states that many years ago General Harlan marched two thousand Bactrian camels four hundred miles, crossed the Indian Caucasus in ice and snow, and lost only one animal, and that by an accident.

The strongest proof that this is a beast made to endure not heat but cold, not the hot sands but the frozen snows, is the method of management adopted by the Mongol owners of the herds. 'Nothing will induce an experienced Mongol to undertake a journey on camels in the hot season,' writes Prejvalski. But from the end of September throughout the winter they cross deep snow, climb mountains, and perform services unequalled by any other animal. They carry tea-chests weighing from four to five hundredweight, can scale passes twelve thousand feet above the sea-level—Prejvalski's camels crossed eight of these in a journey of six hundred and sixty miles—and are driven in carts and ridden. In summer they are watered every forty-eight hours, in winter they can do without water for eight days. They are not only hardy, but long-lived. A Mongol camel begins to earn his living at four years old, and will carry the same burden until from twenty-five to thirty. Some live to be useful for some years beyond this limit. In the tea caravans from Kalgan the camels make two journeys each winter, and earn seven pounds per camel. As most of their food is picked up *en route*, this leaves a good profit to the Mongol owners. Though these camels are owned in hundreds of thousands by the tribes of Central Asia, and are constantly in movement by the caravan routes, the direction of them is almost universally from East to West, or West to East, and the caravans do not enter China beyond the limits of the steppe. This accounts for their being out of touch with all English trade and travel, and renders it difficult to understand whence Mr. Hagenbeck can get as many as he pleases. The answer is—at Tiflis. This is the terminus of the caravan route, and the present Western limit of the wanderings of the Bactrian camel. There they come in thousands every year, arriving in the depth of winter, and leaving before the snows melt on the southern slope of the Caucasus. There, after the caravans have unloaded, the camels can be bought cheap, and be shipped from the Black Sea coast, to which they are brought either by rail or road.

II.—GOATS IN CITIES

THE number of milch-goats exhibited at the last Dairy Show was larger by one-half than has been entered in former years. Many of the animals were highly bred and very handsome creatures, and the quantity and richness of their milk was greater, relatively to their size, even than that of the best Jersey cows. The larger number shown were of the English, Nubian, and Toggenberg breeds. The finest and most domesticated of all, the goats of Syria, were not represented; but those from the herds of Lady Burdett-Coutts and Sir Humphrey de Trafford, President of the British Goat Association—some black and tan, others pale-fawn colour, though with very 'goaty' yellow eyes, and others of broken colour, but with fine glossy coats—were all well adapted for modern use in England. It is claimed that the goat is now qualified to be a 'dairy animal' as much as the cow, that in Germany five goats are kept to every hundred of the human population, and that for poor people, who in rural districts have the greatest difficulty in getting a supply of cow's milk for themselves and their families, or for persons living in towns who require fresh milk for children, the goat is the ideal domestic animal.

It seems probable that in the course of some four thousand years we have reached a point in civilization in which the goat, for ages discredited, finds its place at last. There is nothing in the primitive history of the breed to contradict this view; wild goats are no wilder than wild sheep. But what the old naturalists quaintly called the 'moral' differences between sheep and goats, now known as differences of temperament surviving under domestication, are inexplicable. Both the wild goats and the wild sheep frequent by choice exactly the same regions. That uniformly unattractive and sterile belt of mountain ranges where trees and continuous herbage cease to grow, and only tufts and morsels of vegetation are found, wherever, in fact, there is the maximum of rock and the minimum of food, is the natural haunt of wild goats and wild sheep alike. There are exceptions, such as the markhoor of the Himalayas, which enters the forest belt; but the above holds good of both species when wild, whether in Corsica, Algeria, Persia, the Taurus range, Cyprus, or the Rocky Mountains. Yet the sheep, while preserving its hardy habits when desired, as in the case of all the 'heather sheep' of Exmoor, Wales and

Scotland, adapts itself to rich pasture and artificial feeding, and acquires the temperament, as well as the digestion, of domestication. The goats, as a rule, acquire neither; and though among their various breeds there are exceptions, the English goat is not among them. It remains, just as in the days of old Greece, the enemy of trees, uncontained by fences or walls, inquisitive, pugnacious, restless and omnivorous. It is so unsuited for the settled life of the English farm, that rich pasture makes it ill, and a good clay soil, on which cattle grow fat, soon kills it. But the goat is far from being disqualified for the service of modern civilization by these survivals of primitive habits. Though it cannot live comfortably in the smiling pastures of the low country, it is perfectly willing to exchange the rocks of the mountain for a stable-yard in town. Its love for stony places is amply satisfied by the granite pavement of a 'mews,' and it has been ascertained that goats fed in stalls and allowed to wander in paved yards and courts, live longer and enjoy better health than those tethered even on light pastures with frequent changes of food. In parts of New York the city-kept goats are said to flourish on the paste-daubed paper of the advertisements which they nibble from the hoardings. It is beyond doubt that these hardy creatures are exactly suited for living in large towns. Bricks and mortar and paving-stones exhilarate them. Their spirits rise in proportion to what we should consider the depressing nature of their surroundings. They love to be tethered on a common, with scanty grass and a stock of furze-bushes to nibble. A deserted brickfield, with plenty of broken drain-tiles, rubbish-heaps and weeds, pleases them still better; but the run of a London stable and stable-yard gives them as much satisfaction as the 'liberty' of a mountain-top. They give quantities of excellent milk when kept in this way, are never sick or 'sorry,' and keep the horses interested and free from ennui by their constant visits to the stalls in search of food.

Not even the pig has so varied a diet as the goat. It consumes and converts into milk not only great quantities of garden stuff which would otherwise be wasted, but also, thanks to its love for eating twigs and shoots, it enjoys the prunings and loppings of bushes and trees, which would not be offered to other domestic animals, but which the goat looks upon as exquisite dainties. In old Greece it destroyed the vines, and in modern Greece it has killed off every young tree and bush on the hills till it has disforested the greater part of the Peloponnesus. But the same appetite can be satisfied from an English garden by giving to the goats all the hedge-trimmings, even those of the thorn fences of which cyclists complain so bitterly, and all the prunings of the apple, pear and

GOATS IN A TIMBER-YARD.

plum trees. Feeding goats in their stall or yard is as amusing as feeding the wild ibexes at the Zoo. They will stand on their hind-legs and beg, and when they do obtain the coveted morsel, eat it in a very dainty and well-bred manner. The list of their ordinary food when stall-fed includes potatoes, mangolds, turnips, cabbage-stumps, which they like particularly, as being woody and tough, artichokes, beans, lettuces run to seed, and even dead leaves swept up in autumn, horse-chestnuts and acorns, especially after they have sprouted. Most weeds are eaten by goats, while ivy, and even the long-leaved water-hemlock, which will kill a cow, do not hurt them. When kept in towns, they give large quantities of milk if fed on oats, hay and bean-meal; and in the Mont d'Or district in France they are supplied with oatmeal porridge. With this varied range of diet and plenty of salt, the goat is scarcely ever ill, never suffers from tuberculosis (so that young children are far safer from risk of contracting consumption when fed on goats' milk than on that of cows), and will often give of this milk ten times its own weight in a year.

In our temperate climate, and on the growing quantity of small 'parcels' of land spoilt by building and town areas, there is probably room for as many goats as the patrons of the British Goat Society could desire, even though the conditions are not the same as those in Switzerland, Italy and Greece, where they form an important part of the livestock. That they would have been used here in very early times, had really good breeds been obtainable, as a 'second string' to the dairy, seems evident from the old custom of milking ewes, practised as late as Camden's time on Canvey Island at the mouth of the Thames.

Mr. Lockwood Kipling considers that the goat is a thoroughly Mahommedan beast, and quotes a saying of Mahomet : 'There is no house possessing a goat but a blessing abideth therein ; and there is no house possessing three goats but the angels pass the night praying there.' The British Goat Society are right in desiring that these advantages shall not be limited to Moslems. But far the best breeds belong to the East, and it is strange that the Crusaders never brought back some of the really first-class goats of Palestine and Syria to this country. The difference between the best breeds of sheep and goats of Palestine is far less than might be supposed from the wording of the New Testament. Both have pendulous ears, both are often black in colour, and both follow the shepherd in place of being driven. The goats of Syria are the best of all. The hair is long, with good close under-wool ; they are perfectly domesticated, and are excellent milkers. Instead of sending his milk round to customers in a can or cart, the Syrian dairyman leads his obedient flock of goats down the street, and after receiving an affirmative answer to the Syriac equivalent for the call of 'Milk-ho?' selects his goat, and milks it in the street before the customer's door. If the purchaser fancies milk from one animal more than another he has only to mention his preference.

The Cashmere shawls made of the finest goat's hair are not manufactured from that of Cashmere goats pastured, as is often believed, near the rose-gardens 'where the nightingales sing by the calm Bendemeer.' The precious wool is the under-fur of a breed kept in Thibet, and by the Khirgiz in Central Asia, from the slopes of the Alatau Mountains to the bend of the Ural north of the Caspian. Only a small quantity, averaging three ounces, of the precious wool is produced yearly by each goat, and the material is collected by middlemen, taken to Cashmere and sold in the bazaars, where it is purchased by the makers of the shawls. M. Jaubert in 1819 imported some of these animals into France, and after crossing them with the Angora breed, obtained an average of thirty ounces instead of three ounces of equally fine wool. Recent experiments in acclimatizing the vicuna in France have met with considerable success, and both the Cashmere and Angora goats were found to do well on the Swiss Alps, though as they gave no milk they were not popular with the farmer. Welcome as a new form of butcher's meat would be in England, the flesh of the goat, or even of kids, has never been highly praised; but there is a future for the goat as a minor dairy animal both in villages and towns.

III.—THE 'NEW' PIG

Recent Agricultural Returns, encouraging in other respects, disclose a very sad falling-off in the pig population of the United Kingdom. In 1897 there was a decrease of more than half a million, and though it is maintained that the figures do not include those kept on 'occupations' of less than half an acre, and should not be taken to heart too seriously by the great number of persons interested in pigs, either as objects of pleasure or profit, there is no doubt that they are temporarily under a cloud. In the phrase of the market, 'pigs are quiet,' and unless the price of grain continues to drop they are likely to remain so for some time.

Nothing could be more timely, in this partial eclipse of an animal so long and justly prized, than the appearance of Mr. Saunders Spencer's treatise on modern pigs,* which not only does full justice to their many admirable qualities, but also gives a very interesting account of their recent history and development, and treats their

* 'Pigs: their Breeds and Management.' By Saunders Spencer. London: Vinton and Co.

idiosyncrasies, whether in health or disease, with a sober and serious sympathy which is highly practical and, incidentally, most entertaining. The history and improvement of our famous breeds of cattle is a grander theme; it deals with archaic types, ancestral herds, and the efforts and expenditure of great landed proprietors. The story of our pigs runs on a humbler level. The peasant, and not the great proprietor, has raised the modern pig to its present perfection. Its recent development limits its interest to the naturalist. There is a lack of individuality in the appearance of different breeds of British pigs. Any stranger who visits the Smithfield Cattle Show is struck with the great variety of shape, colour, and size in the cattle 'classes.' But to appreciate the differences in pigs one must be 'in the fancy,' except in the case of a few breeds which retain traces of colour or form due to ancient environment. Thus Mr. Spencer mentions with disapproval an aquatic and detrimental pig which formerly haunted the Fens and the valley of the Ouse. Some of these may still be found in parts of the Fens 'far removed from railways or the beneficial influence of a good herd of pure-bred pigs.' The 'Tamworths' are the offspring of what are commonly believed to be the original forest pigs which Gurth the swineherd fed for Cedric the Saxon. They hailed originally from the 'Ivanhoe' country near Sherwood Forest, whither they were sent in droves in autumn from the country round, just as they were in the New Forest. These pigs were rufous, sandy, or mahogany coloured animals, just matching the dead leaves of beech and oak in autumn and early winter. In the beginning of the century the Forest was rapidly enclosed, and the farmers found that the independent pig, who expected his autumn holiday regularly, and 'saw that he got it,' by breaking out of his sty and taking to the woods, was rather troublesome. So they crossed him most appropriately with the Neapolitan pig, who is the laziest of all pigs, and produced the Tamworth, a 'golden' pig, resembling the forest swine in shape and colour, but having the love for the *dolce far niente* inherited from his Neapolitan ancestors. Berkshire pigs, the 'large white pigs,' originally bred in Yorkshire, middle whites, and small whites, complete the pedigree list, and it is interesting to note that, though few in number, they are unequalled in quality. England has provided Berkshire pigs for the model farms of the Austrian Government in Bosnia and Herzegovina. It has exported Tamworths and 'large whites' to Argentina, Illinois, and the Sandwich Islands, and reclaimed by intermixture many relapsed and imperfect breeds of pigs in Germany and Austria.

In England, during recent years, the great ham question has much enhanced the difficulties of breeders. To produce an animal from whose body good bacon can be made, and whose legs are perfect for hams, has been found almost beyond the resources of art. Even Mr. Saunders Spencer admits that to adumbrate the proportions of the 'perfect pig' is beyond the scope of his imagination, and to hope to produce one in the concrete is to strive after the unattainable. The omission of all the half-acre plots from the Agricultural Returns casts a slur on a very highly esteemed and numerous class, the 'backyard' pigs. There are, it is believed, more pigs kept in cottage-gardens and back-yards in the North than in farms. But after making every allowance for omissions, the United Kingdom makes a poor figure compared with the United States. One year with another, we rear three million pigs. In the maize-growing States of the Union the present number is estimated at forty millions, and this is thirteen millions less than the highest figure reached by the pig population of the States. The number of pigs kept by the colliers and artisans of the North fluctuates with the price of coal and yarn. In good times every collier keeps a live animal of some sort, and, though dogs, guinea-pigs, cage-birds, and homing-pigeons are attractive, his 'fancy animal' is usually a pig. He admires this on Sunday afternoons, and groups of friends go round to smoke their pipes and compare pigs, and bet on their ultimate weight. They have private pig-shows, with subscription prizes. Each animal is judged in its own sty, and it is interesting to know that the evolution of an almost perfect pig was due to the innate sagacity of the Yorkshire pit-hand. The sties in which these animals live are very rough affairs, often made of a few boards nailed over railway-sleepers; but it is interesting to learn that the young pigs are 'as blooming and healthy as possible,' and that, small though the collier's back-yard is, he always contrives that his pig-sty shall be thoroughly ventilated and look towards the south. Architects of costly home-farms often house the unhappy pigs under north walls, and condemn them to rheumatism, cold, and sunlessness.

Yorkshire produces not only the best pork, but has long been famous for the best cured hams in the world. But elsewhere it is curious to note the dislike of the farming class to any form of manufacture other than that of raw material. One-fourth of the English pigs are kept in Norfolk, Suffolk, and Essex. Yet Mr. Saunders Spencer doubts whether there is now a bacon-curing factory in Suffolk, and relates the failure of one established in Norfolk. In the former case, the people would not rear the precise kind of animal wanted; in the latter, the dealers made a ring, and put up prices beyond the margin of profit. Our Illinois is Somersetshire and Wiltshire, and our little Chicago the 'sausage town' of Calne. As almost everyone who has a country house, large or small, is 'interested,' to use the city phrase, in pigs, whether he be squire, parson, farmer, labourer, gardener, policeman, or postman (I believe the village schoolmasters are the only class who scorn to keep a pig), the methods of the Calne factories ought to be more widely known than they are. The animals, in lots of not less than ten, can be sent by rail directly to the factory without extra charge, if the paid distance be less than 100 miles. There they are weighed and classified, and the price calculated directly, with a bonus of two shillings and sixpence on each pig which comes up to a certain standard of merit. This canon of perfection was evolved at Calne, the result of a wide experience of the needs of the curers, and the shortcomings of 'fashionable' pigs. Since then it has become a standard —the rule of Pigdom—to which all its members must conform, or become pork instead of bacon, and end their lives as failures.

Mr. Spencer suggests one further interesting question in connection with his subject, but he does not pursue it. 'When wages are lower, the price of pigs is higher,' he remarks, 'because the farm-labourers and artisans consume a greater quantity of pork, and less beef and mutton.' What would Cobbett, who saw the maximum of a labourer's well-being in a plentiful supply of pork, bread, and beer, say to this advance, by which that sound, and then all too scarce, fare now takes the second or third place in the scale of the workman's diet? 'Salt pork,' which was for centuries the staple food of the mariners of England, is almost erased from the bill of fare on passenger ships, and is only served twice a week to the bluejackets in the navy. Before long mere salted pig will be as antiquated as stock fish or 'poor John.' It only holds its place as a humble necessary of life among American backwoodsmen. Even they have recently 'struck' against the quality of that supplied from Chicago, and demanded a more 'matured' article for winter diet.

But the English-reared pig is no longer the poor man's food-animal. On the contrary, it is a luxury. New Zealand mutton, La Plata beef, Columbian salmon, and Australian rabbits, are the cheap form of fresh meat, and by many classes, notably respectable domestic servants, home-grown pork is preferred to any of these. It is dearer actually and relatively, for more is eaten at a meal. Nearly all the fresh pig sold in this country may be considered to be the flesh of highly-bred and highly-fed animals. But the English bacon and English hams are the product of highly-skilled manufacture. It is not long since bacon was considered only fit for ploughmen; it never appeared at a gentleman's breakfast-table; even in farmhouses it was only eaten as a domestic duty. This was no prejudice; the pigs were bad, and the bacon worse:

it was salt, strong, and often rancid. Now it is more difficult to buy bad bacon or ill-cured hams than it was formerly to buy them of good quality. The best is found on the breakfast-tables of all classes, while the Bradenham and Yorkshire hams figure on their merits in city banquets.

IV.—THE STORY OF THE JERSEY HERD

Among the highest prices made for Jersey cattle during the last two years were those at the sale of a herd at New Park, in the New Forest.* These island cattle made an average of £28 each, though some of those sold were only calves a few weeks old, and one heifer was purchased for fifty-one guineas. Though nothing could be more thoroughly English than the scene under the New Forest oaks, as the little cattle left their beds of fern and strolled one by one into the 'ring,' it was remarked that of all our domestic cattle, these are the only creatures in this country which are in all respects comparable in temper and beauty with the best domestic breeds of India. The resemblance consists not in form, which is different from the 'humped' Oriental breeds, but in the satin fineness of their coats, the golden bronze, silver gray, and other 'Quaker' hues common also to the smaller Indian cow, and the perfect friendliness with man which these petted

* A Jersey cow sold very recently at a sale near Brighton for a hundred and twenty guineas.

creatures have inherited from generations of kind treatment. As each strolled into the sale-ring, it walked up to any spectator who took its fancy, and pushed its muzzle out to be patted, or put its head up to be stroked, with a confidence which scarcely any other breed of domesticated animal would show if suddenly brought into the company of a crowd of unknown human beings. Their eyes were black, their eyelashes long and silky, all their noses were fringed with a narrow silver edging of satin hair, and their skin, where it showed elsewhere, was covered with a yellow bloom, of the correct 'butter-pat' tint, which suffused the very hollows of their high-bred ears.

The story of the Jersey herd should have belonged to an earlier age. They are, as an island race, the modern equivalent of the cattle of the Sun, the earliest of all pedigree herds, which fed on sea-washed Trinacria; and there is something so contrary to probability in their first beginnings, that it seems to need a setting in legend. Treated as a fact in natural history, it will be allowed that conditions less likely to develop a species to perfection could scarcely be found than those on a small island, eleven and a half miles long and five miles wide, set in a stormy, narrow sea.

Limited space, exposure to sea gales, and the tendency to interbreed, together with the absence of any surplus of natural food, and the difficulty of importing it when steamers were unknown, and the usual means of access was by small cutters crossing a dangerous sea, were all natural difficulties in the way of such a result. Had the nucleus of the herd been formed by some accidental deposit of cattle of marked excellence on these Channel islets, their isolation would doubtless have helped to preserve the breed pure. But there is reason to believe that the Jersey cattle were, in their origin, of the same kind as those on the neighbouring mainland of Brittany. Mr. John Thornton, the compiler of the 'English Herd-Book of Jersey Cattle,' has some very interesting speculations on the wider question of the descent of the small breed, originally black and white, or black, to which they have most affinity. This breed is noted as being best known and most numerous in those parts of France and the British Islands where the population is of Celtic origin and Druidical remains are most common. Such a race is found in Brittany, near Carnac, in Kerry, and was formerly common in Cornwall. With these may be compared the ancient British cattle kept in Badminton Park; and in Anglesea, 'that ancient and peculiar seat of Druidical superstition,' Youatt noted that the old breed of cattle was 'small and black.' On this Mr. Thornton founds the very ingenious conclusion that 'if the shorthorns represent the improved type of the "bos urus," or wild white cattle of Chillingham, so the Jersey cattle and their relations are the most improved type of the "bos longifrons," or smaller domesticated race.' It remains to be shown how little 'Druidical' cows bred on an islet have not deteriorated like Shetland ponies or Iceland cows, but have developed into the creatures now eagerly bought not only by English gentlemen and English country ladies, for the Jerseys are pre-eminently 'ladies' cows,' but in North America, Germany, South Africa, Australia, New Zealand, and recently in Brazil, where some, lately imported, walked two hundred miles through the forest, and arrived in good condition at their destination. The history of the breed in the Jersey Herd-Book gives no *a priori* theory for this process, but we incline to think that it has a natural explanation. The people were industrious and intensely practical. The area which they inhabited was very small, and though the population was large, every part of the little island, and every cow on it, might well be familiar, either in fact or by reputation, to every possible purchaser of cattle on the spot. Being all neighbours, and knowing the merits or failings of each other's cattle, a bad cow had no chance of finding a purchaser, and its calves went to the butcher. 'Natural selection' was at work in this case through the agency of man. Then the inhabitants of the island caught, quite early in the last century, a violent fit of the 'cow-fancying' mania, which Hindoos have magnified into a form of worship, though its broad basis is their passion for the animal itself. Early in this century this exclusive devotion moved the wrath of Thomas Quayle. 'The treatment of sheep and horses,' he wrote, 'is almost a disgrace to Jersey agriculture. The treasure highest in a Jersey man's estimation is his cow. She seems to be the constant object of his thoughts and attention; and that attention she certainly deserves.... In summer she must submit to be staked to the ground. But five or six times a day her station is shifted. In winter she is warmly housed by night, and fed with the precious parsnip. When she calves she is regaled with toast and cider, the nectar of the island, to which powdered ginger is added.'

The Jerseymen, who had only twenty-nine thousand acres of arable land in their whole island, had been clever enough to discover the root which of all others is most suitable for milch cows; and their parsnip-growing made possible for them as great strides in the development of their breed as that of the turnip did for the general stock of English cattle. Next to improving their own cattle they were most eager to keep out all others. Their indignation when they suspected that inferior Brittany animals were about to be imported, or might be sold as the produce of the island, finds expression in various old statutes. An Act passed in 1789 condemned anyone importing cattle from France to a fine of £200 per head; the ship was to be confiscated, the cattle killed, and the meat sold for the poor of the parish where it was seized. In 1826, when the great and valuable export trade was established, the fine was raised to £1,000 per head of cattle introduced, with confiscation of the vessel, and this might be seized, and the fine imposed, if it were within two leagues of the shore.

The motive for this intense vigilance will be found in the great profits drawn by the island from the English 'discovery' of Channel Island cattle. The first imported came from Alderney, where there was a garrison. The little cows came over as 'camp followers,' and attracted little notice. They were called 'Alderneys,' and later, 'Alderney Jerseys.' The first person to note them as qualified for the highest circles of bovine society was a Yorkshireman, Mr. Fowler, the travelling partner in a large London dairy. In 1811 he saw one coming home unsold from a fair, and bought it for his wife, and took it to his home at Little Bushey. The despised little cow gave such enormous quantities of butter and cream that her new master inquired her origin, and soon began to import the breed wholesale from the islands. His son managed the transit, had the herds *shod* with thin iron plates when they reached Southampton, and sold them mainly in the home counties. It was no easy matter to ship them, though the cattle, as tame as dogs from their daily handling and feeding fastened to the chain, gave no trouble. They were brought over in the Channel cutters, the other cargo usually consisting of cider. One boat was thirteen days out, and the captain, running short of water, tapped the cider casks. The cows enjoyed it so much that for three days they would drink nothing else. The steps by which system and method have been introduced into the cult of the Jersey herd belong to the history of the English Jersey Herd Society and the Royal Jersey Agricultural Society. The pedigree herds have multiplied until there is not a county in England where they may not be found, and the produce are scattered in twos and threes in the paddocks of half the country houses in England. But it is in Jersey itself, not in the 'adjacent island' of Great Britain, that the most suggestive results of the possession of the Jersey herd are to be noted. Note the cultivated area: twenty-nine thousand acres, or eleven thousand acres less than is owned by one nobleman in Norfolk. Add the same amount of uncultivated ground, and we have the total available raw material for agriculture in the island. This maintained in 1880 nearly eleven thousand Jersey cattle, two thousand two hundred and sixty-one horses, three hundred and forty-six sheep, five thousand eight hundred and forty-four pigs. The total population was sixty thousand, half of whom live in St. Heliers. But the total value of the cattle and potatoes exported in the one year of 1879 was somewhat above £350,000. No doubt the early spring gives the Jersey men an advantage in the vegetable market. But the value of the cattle is not due to chance. The two most prosperous agricultural areas in Great Britain are both islands—Jersey and Anglesea. Why cannot the Isle of Wight be a rival?

V.—THE CAT ABOUT TOWN

That the cat still maintains its position as the best mouse-catching machine procurable is shown by its increase in great towns. The number of London cats, according to a writer in the *Daily Mail*, is 400,000, of which half are 'unattached,' and live largely on refuse, 'because London is the most wasteful city in the world.' As London is also one of the cleanest cities in the world, it is very doubtful if the waste food comes much in the way of the unattached London cat, who, like other Metropolitan paupers, levies handsome contributions on kind-hearted people, whose doorsteps and areas it besets, and also catches numbers of pigeons, sparrows, rats, and mice, the three last of which do live on London refuse, which the cat eats in the more convenient form of cold sparrow or mouse. Evidence quoted by the writer shows that this is so, for he states that in most parts of London the rats have been driven underground into the sewers by the warfare of the cats. He also holds that the latter are somewhat changing in character, are losing their dislike of water and wet, and prefer to be out in the rain. We rather doubt these conclusions, and believe that if the London cat differs at all from his country cousin, it is in selecting different hours for his sport and amusements. The country cat is more or less lively all day, and hunts regularly in the evening. The London cat is sleepy and quiet all day, because circumstances make him a very early riser, or, at any rate, prevent him having his morning sleep. The explanation of the languor and *ennui* of the London cat is to be found in the fact that long before he appears at the breakfast-table, with a jaded appetite and a general air of aloofness from the world and its pleasures, he has had a long morning's sport, often in delightful society, and then breakfasted comfortably in the kitchen. The scenes of these early-morning hunts are various, and the hour during half the year is one before even the earliest of early risers are about. In winter the London cats often seek their sport under cover. In one district near a very large and famous brewery the sporting cats go regularly as soon as the brewery gates are open to hunt rats in the brewery 'stores.' This is capital fun, as there are hundreds of barrels, either stored or 'working,' with little patches of yeasty froth oozing from the bungholes and plenty of dropped corn and 'grains' in the neighbourhood to attract all the rats from elsewhere. Under and among these barrels they may be hunted with success for an hour or more. Besides the brewery rats, which are said to drink beer when they can get it, there are 'temperance rats,' which live by the river, and, so far as we know, only drink water. These form the grand objects of summer sport to all London cats in range of the Thames, from the docks in the east to Chiswick in the west, and all along the old muddy foreshore on the Surrey side, where no embankment intervenes to spoil sport. We have never heard of an instance of London cats catching fish by the river, probably because until very recently there have been so few fish to catch. But the keenness of the cats for this riverside hunting by the tidal Thames is such that they often return covered and clotted with mud from the foreshore, where they have either fallen in from the wharves, or have pursued a rat escaping across the leavings of the river ebb.

In summer mornings, from 4 a.m. to about 5 a.m., London ceases for the moment to belong to the world of men, and for the moment is given up to the sole enjoyment of the London birds and the London cats. At this really bewitching hour, for the town is quite beautiful then, the cats may be seen, as at no other time, monarchs of all they survey — *rerum domini*, masters of the town. Then it may be seen that it is not for nothing that the race have for generations maintained their independence, and asserted their right to roam. For at that hour *all the dogs are shut up;* all the boys and grown-up people, too, are asleep. There is not even a milkman about, or an amalgamated engineer going to his before-breakfast work. The city is theirs. Their demeanour at this time is absolutely changed. They stroll about the streets and gardens with an air. They converse in the centre of highways. They walk with a certain feline *abandon* and momentary magnificence over gardens and squares. For the time they are not cats, but lions and tigers ; or, to change the simile, they are no longer domestics, but gentlemen at large. Before sunrise one midsummer morning the writer was watching the early birds by the side of the London river, and wondering at the abundance and variety of life in the silver-gray light of the dawn. A pair of water-hens were running on the mud left by the ebb, sedge-warblers singing, as they had done all night, and a pair of turtle-doves flew down to drink before sunrise. When the first beams of the sun sent long shafts of light down the river, the sedge-warblers were instantly silent ; and almost immediately the blackbirds and sparrows and starlings appeared upon the grass. At this moment another ornithologist appeared upon the scene in the person of an elegant young female cat. She made great efforts to stalk the fat blackbirds and cock-sparrows, flattening herself till her whole body seemed almost as level as a mat, yet

THE CAT AS WILD ANIMAL.

capable of a rush forward whenever the birds looked in another direction. But the birds were perfectly equal to the game. One blackbird in particular sidled off each time the cat came within distance, until he sat at last on the edge of the wooden cam-shedding, where, if the cat made her spring, she must fall into the river. He, too, flew off, and at this moment of disappointment another and an older cat leapt lightly from the privet hedge close by and playfully cuffed the head of the disappointed one. This cat had probably been waiting on the chance of a 'drive' while the more impetuous one tried a stalk in the open. The latter seemed half inclined to resent the humorous turn which the older cat gave to her hunting; but the two soon made it up, and, after strolling ostentatiously across the lawn with their tails up, separated, and the young one adjourned to hunt 'ground-game' in the cam-shedding. The quarry were either mice or rats, but were attacked by storm, and not by waiting. The cat dived her paws into the cracks of the boards, reaching in as far as her shoulders, and soon bolted something, which she reached after head downwards so far that nothing but her tail and one hind-paw were visible. After hanging almost head downwards for some time, she scrambled back, just as the first cat came darting past like a wild animal with an enormous rat in its mouth.

It is doubtful whether the London cat is in the least

degree more docile or *biddable* than his country cousin. He is more dependent on man, for no one ever hears of a London cat going off to live a wild life willingly, though country cats do this frequently. It has been observed of the whole race, at least in this country, that though they will often obey the order 'Come,' they absolutely refuse to entertain the command 'Go ;' and as most useful service involves this as the initial idea, the animal which refuses obedience to it is practically useless except as a volunteer. The admirable sporting qualities, even of the London cat, should make him a most useful and amusing aid in sport, if he could be induced to co-operate with his owner. There is only one piece of evidence that in ancient times the cat was so trained—an Egyptian painting showing a cat bringing wild-fowl to its master from a papyrus bed—and very few instances are on record even of its being trained to retrieve in our day. A visitor to one of the monasteries on Mount Carmel states that when several of the monks went out, gun on shoulder, to shoot game for the pot, he saw their cats marching out after them, to aid as retrievers; but he did not witness the sport. There is no doubt that cats can be trained to follow, like dogs. A working-man in the North Midlands recently owned a small cat which followed him all day, and when tired was carried in a large pocket in its master's coat. So also a navvy some years ago owned a cat which had followed or accompanied him to work in most parts of North and Western England, sometimes following him on foot and sometimes carried in the white washable bag in which navvies keep their Sunday clothes. But as a rule it is much easier to teach them *not* to do things than to do them. Recently in a large London engineering works there was some regret that the 'best foundry cat' was dead. The sand used for making casts in the foundry is mixed with flour. Mice come to eat the flour and spoil the 'moulds.' It is not desirable that rats and mice should be about in this loft, so cats are kept there. The cats have to be taught not to walk about on the moulds or scratch them up, and this 'best foundry cat' was absolutely perfect in this respect. In these works most departments have a special cat. There is even one in the galvanizing shop which knows quite well that the hot metal spirts when plates are dipped in, and has learnt to get under cover at that juncture. It need scarcely be said that the London cat is a worse enemy to caged birds even than the country pussy, as in the daytime it lives more indoors. Whether it ever catches gold-fish out of a bowl we do not know, but there are no complaints of its robbing fishmongers' shops to gratify its taste in that line. On the whole, we imagine that the cat is happy in London, far happier, for instance, than the dog. Even if lost, he has much more *savoir faire* than the latter. The stray dog attaches himself to someone in the street, who has at once the uncomfortable feeling that the dog is trying to make out that he has stolen him. The lost cat comes to a house and asks relief where it can most readily be given.

VI.—A 'WOULD-BE' HELPER: THE FRIENDLY PUMA

RECENT inquiry presents the puma, the 'lion' of the New World, in a very pleasing light. It is claimed that the puma is positively friendly to man, hostile to other large carnivora, and that alone of the great cats it desires of its free will to be a 'helper and server' of man. This belief, very strongly asserted by Mr. Hudson in his 'Naturalist in La Plata,' which rests both on the local belief of the inhabitants of a great part of South America, and on the records of the naturalists and historians of the old Spanish colonies, receives some support from an incident recently communicated to the writer by a gentleman on a visit to this country in connection with the Venezuela Boundary Commission, after a long residence in British Guiana. He was going up one of the rivers in a steam-launch, and gave a passage to a Cornish miner who was going up to the gold-fields. The passenger, who was an elderly man, usually slung his hammock on shore. One morning, being asked how he had slept, he complained that the frogs had wakened him by croaking near his hammock. Some Indians, who had been taking down the hammock, laughed, and, being asked the reason, still laughing, said, 'Oh, "tiger" sleep with old man last night.' They had satisfied themselves that a puma had been lying just under the hammock, which was slung low down, and it was probably the satisfied purring of the puma, which had enjoyed the pleasure of sleeping in the 'next berth' below a man, that had wakened the occupant of the hammock.

The beliefs to the credit of the puma, recorded both by ordinary observers and by naturalists—the earliest being Don Felix d'Azara, and the latest Mr. Hudson—fall under three divisions. It is believed to be the friend of man: the Spanish Indians call it *amigo del Christiano*, a nice distinction which cannot be conceded, because the Indians of North California considered the puma a friendly god before the missionaries arrived, and would not molest it. It was also alleged to protect men from other wild animals, particularly from the jaguar, to attack this stronger and more ferocious animal and drive it away, and under no provocation to attack man himself. All three stories so much resemble the medieval fictions about animals, especially the 'feud' between the puma and the jaguar, which is exactly analogous to the myths of the feud between the elephant and the dragon, the deer and the serpent, with many others, that we should hardly expect to see them survive the period of early Jesuit conversion. But, on the contrary, these beliefs, which the Indians held long before they were converted, are now restated in a much more positive form, and with abundance of corroborative evidence. Views only tentatively held, or set down as current, but not confirmed, by Azara, are fully confirmed by Mr. Hudson. Meantime, it is interesting to see exactly what Azara did say, as he is a very intelligent and honourable Spanish gentleman, and 'spent twenty years alone with the birds and wild beasts.' When Don Felix d'Azara was making his notes on the natural history of Paraguay, between 1782 and 1801, he received a copy of Buffon's 'Natural History,' then a new book, and in the acme of its fame. The Spaniard, not dazzled by Buffon's brilliant generalizations, found that his facts as to South American animals were much amiss. 'Vulgar, false, and mistaken,' was Azara's outspoken criticism. He therefore determined to show what a Spaniard could do, working in the field of facts, to do justice to the South American species, or, as he naïvely calls them, '*my* animals—*my* cats, *my* monkeys, *my* otters.' The puma, 'my second species of cat,' then very common in many districts with which Azara was acquainted, though it was almost killed off in Paraguay, was the subject of a very careful essay. This carefulness is the mark of all his work, which, as we have said, was intended to set Buffon right, and to give facts only. He knew that the young were spotted 'like a female jaguar,' and he notes that he had 'never heard that they have assaulted or attempted to attack man, nor boys, nor dogs, even when they encounter them asleep; on the contrary, they run away or conceal themselves, showing fear; and as their speed is inferior to that of a horse, a mounted man easily overtakes them.' He is mistaken as to the dogs, for pumas are sometimes particularly hostile to them. A tame puma, when following its master obediently, has been known to rush through a crowd in chase of a dog. The instances of its tameness in captivity cited by Azara are interesting. A village priest had one raised from a cub, which ran loose like a dog. It was given to Azara, who kept it on a chain, but it 'was as tame as a dog, and very playful.' It played with everyone, and took great delight in licking the skin of his negroes. 'On presenting it with an orange or any other thing, it handled it with its forepaws, playing with it in the same way as a cat does with a mouse. It caught fowls (its one form of mischief) with the same stratagems and cunning as a cat, not omitting the movement of the extremity of its tail. . . . I never saw it irritated. When rubbed or tickled it lay down and purred like a cat. My negroes one day loosed it, and it followed them to the river, traversing the city without even meddling with the dogs in the street.' To these notes of Azara's, his translator, Mr. W. Perceval Hunter, added in 1837 other evidence of its docility. He mentions the puma kept by Kean the tragedian, the skeleton of which is now in the Museum of the Royal College of Surgeons. This used to follow Kean loose in his garden and in his house, and was 'introduced to company in his drawing-room.' He also quotes an account of another tame puma kept in Edinburgh, 'which rejoices greatly in the company of those to whom it is accustomed, lies down upon its back between their feet, and plays with the skirts of their garments entirely after the manner of a kitten.' It got loose in London, but most properly allowed itself to be captured by the watchman—a thing which no animal of spirit ought to have permitted.

The corroborative evidence as to the feud between the puma and the jaguar is most interesting. Azara himself, though he mentions the story, doubts it. He has a sound critical faculty, and pitched at once on a weak point in the belief. The Indians alleged that the female pumas were carried off by jaguars. Hence the ill-feeling. This, he says, is clearly nonsense. But this 'gloss' can, we think, be accounted for. The puma cubs are spotted, some more distinctly than others, at birth, though the puma, *felis concolor*, is without spots. Hence the story of the jaguar cross. The main belief appears constantly. A Spanish girl who was tied to a tree by the Spanish Governor of Buenos Ayres for visiting the Indians avowed that a puma had sat by her all night, and driven the other beasts (jaguars) away. This was regarded as a miracle; but Mr. Hudson declares that it would not now excite surprise. 'It is well known that where the two species inhabit the same district they are at enmity, the puma being the persistent persecutor of the jaguar, following and harassing it as the "tyrant bird" does the eagle, and, when an opportunity occurs, springing upon its back and inflicting terrible wounds with its teeth and claws. Jaguars with scarred backs are frequently killed, and others not long escaped from their tormentors have been found greatly lacerated.' This *might* have been done by fights with other jaguars, but in support of the general belief of the gauchos, who spend their lives on the pampas where these species are common, two pieces of evidence are quoted. One, that a similar dislike for other carnivora on the part of the puma is current in a far-distant region—North California—where it is said to attack the grizzly bear. The second was communicated to Mr. Hudson, after a hunt in which one of the very rare instances of a puma trying to defend itself from a man occurred. A gaucho had tried to kill a puma, as if it were a sheep, with his knife, and the animal, after dodging the first blow, had struck him in the face with his paw. In a previous hunt (after game and ostriches) one of their company had fallen from his horse and broken his leg. He lay on the pampa all night, and when found next morning told the following story. An hour after it became dark a puma came and sat by him. After frequently going and returning, it left him for a long time. About midnight he heard the roar of a jaguar, and gave himself up for lost. But the jaguar was watching something else. It moved out of sight, and he then heard snarls and growls, and the sharp cry of a puma, and knew that the two beasts were fighting. The jaguar returned several times, and the puma renewed the contest every time until morning, when both disappeared. Mr. Hudson had 'already met with many anecdotes of a similar kind in various parts of the country, some vastly more interesting than this. But he gave this account because it was at first hand.' Many instances are given by Mr. Hudson of the puma's confidence in man. He also gives three cases of its refusal to defend itself, and another in which four pumas played round a sleeping man for several hours at night without disturbing him. The Southern puma is the animal credited with these friendly instincts. In North America it has been much persecuted by man, and bears a different character. But in Argentina, in 'places where the puma is the only large beast of prey, it is notorious that it is perfectly safe for even a small child to go out and sleep on the plain.' Yet among other animals the puma is courageous and destructive. It is a desperate sheep-killer, a destroyer of foals, 'a peregrine falcon among mammals.' Such an instinct of friendliness in a big cat, unique, and the more surprising because even when domesticated the race rarely exhibits more than an equable and distant tolerance of man's existence, will no doubt attract the attention of those who have the opportunity of collecting information at first hand in the plains of South America. No one but reliable 'field-naturalists,' ranch-owners, and sportsmen can do so, and for these it should form an interesting object of inquiry.

VII.—ANIMAL COLONISTS

AMONG instances of successful acclimatization of English animals in the Antipodes must be reckoned the importation of red deer into New Zealand. They were first introduced in 1862, when Prince Albert, to oblige the Government Agent of New Zealand in London, caused four stags and two hinds to be shipped to Wellington. Only one stag and two hinds arrived alive, and were set free on Taratahi Plains. They selected for their haunt a range of limestone hills, covered with good English grasses, and there they have flourished and multiplied abundantly. During the last four years the effects of this increase have been noted in the appearance of the deer in every locality near which wood, water, and grass are plentiful. Licenses for deer-shooting, limited to three stags a season, have been issued for the last ten years. The stags grow faster than in England, bearing antlers with ten points in three years, and some of the numerous calves are being captured and transferred to other districts as stock. Other red deer are also about to be imported, not from England, but from Australia, these being of English stock 'once removed.'

This is only a minor and recent instance of what we may term the colonizing faculty of English animals. They seem to share the physical, and in some degree the mental, capacity of the British for 'getting on' in new countries, and to make more of their opportunities than the indigenous creatures, without possessing such marked advantages as their masters often have over the human inhabitants. If a census could be taken of the creatures of British descent making up the animal population in the vast new territories peopled by men of English blood, the world would contemplate with astonishment the facts of this double migration and dual increase of man and beast alike from two small islands in the West Atlantic. Nor do our animal colonists confine themselves to the new Anglo-Saxon countries. Whatever unkindly criticisms are levelled at the Englishman abroad, the English animals, domesticated and wild, are everywhere welcome. The sparrow and the rabbit are the two exceptions which prove the rule; but for almost every other British animal, from Derby winners and pedigree shorthorns to Norfolk pheasants and Loch Leven trout, the men of the New World, the colonists of Great Britain, Spain, Portugal, and even of Holland—for the Boers are now

UNWELCOME COLONISTS.

purchasing British cattle—compete in lavish expenditure in their zeal for an inheritance in the beasts, birds, and fishes of our good country.

This colonization by animals has had a settled order of time, corresponding fairly closely with the social evolution of the British and foreign possessions to which they have been involuntary migrants. The 'pioneer animals,' like the first colonists, have often been rather a 'rough lot.' Times were bad after the great war, and our farmers did not own one-twentieth part of the fine pedigree stock now so plentiful in this country. But the first colonizing animals had to be of the useful sort, beasts of burden or for food, if not the best, then the best which could be got. So the settlers in Australia, the backwoods of Canada, and Cape Colony and Natal, had for their first animal population a prolific and hardy, but not a high-bred class of English stock. There were abundance of sheep, of cattle, of fowls, and some British horses. The ancestors of the animal colonists of New Zealand, now represented by twenty millions of sheep and cattle alone, were imported later, and from more carefully selected stock, than those first taken to the older colonies. Meantime, the latter had reached the stage of prosperity in which it pays not only to possess many flocks and herds, but also to have them of high quality. Sheep, cattle, and horses were improved by the best English blood that money could

4—2

buy, as well as by the importation of the merino sheep from Spain, with which the English breeds were crossed; and, by a fortunate coincidence, the time at which Australasia desired an accession of quality to quantity in her British-descended stock corresponded with a period of extraordinary activity and success in the breeding and development of pedigree cattle, sheep, horses, and swine by the 'landed interest,' owners and tenants alike, in this country. We need not follow this, the greatest and most obvious invasion of the New World by the host of British animals, beyond the facts conveyed in the sum-total of the numbers of the three most necessary, and therefore most numerous, classes—the sheep, cattle, and horses, the two latter being mainly, if not entirely, of British descent—owned by the colonies of Australia and New Zealand. The figures are, in round numbers, one hundred and eleven millions of sheep, nine millions of cattle, and one million three hundred thousand horses. Except the merino sheep, the Angora goat, and the camel, recently introduced into West Australia, we believe that there is no domesticated animal in Australia which is not of English stock. Numbers must be considered first, if justice is to be done to the magnitude of this animal movement from West to East; but, apart from counting heads, the list of British species entirely omitted from the totals given above, but now firmly established in the New World, is no less striking. All other domesticated forms—pigs, all breeds of English dogs, prize poultry, and pigeons, in as great variety and perfection as they attain in this country—are equally established in Australasia, and with them the red deer, the pheasant, the trout, and, unfortunately, the rabbit and the sparrow. In Australia, and still more noticeably in New Zealand, the new-comers, the most vigorous representatives of the later types of animal, had a clear advantage over the ancient marsupial forms and the wingless birds. The pheasant, which can both run and fly, displaces the New Zealand apteryx, and the rabbit gets the better of the wallaby and smaller kangaroos.

But while the British animals, with the aid of their owners, were displacing the native creatures of Australasia, they were achieving a parallel success in another continent, and among a population who cannot be suspected of any preferential leanings towards the animals of these islands. The Spanish Republics of South America were rapidly 'Anglicizing' their flocks and herds, originally descended and inherited from pure Spanish stock. In Argentina the demand for British-bred animals first arose among the flockmasters, though cattle-raising was the earlier and national occupation. But the improvement in wool effected by introducing the best English breeds was rapid and obvious, while that in the form and quality of the cattle was a slower process. But during the last few years the demand for pedigree English cattle for Argentina has been enormous. Shorthorns, Herefords, and Devons have been imported weekly, and a cross-bred English stock now fills the 'corrals' of the great beef and bovril companies of the River Plate. In North America this Anglicizing process has spread to all the States of the Union. Half-bred Herefords and shorthorns are taking the place of the common cattle of the States on nearly all the ranches of the beef-producing districts, and the colonizing capacity of different English breeds is recommending them for special districts. Thus the Devon bulls are purchased for ranches where the search for pasture and water needs special activity and endurance, and red 'polled' or hornless Suffolks are used where cattle are being bred for transit by rail or ship, because the absence of horns is then convenient. Even tropical Brazil follows the fashion, and English Jersey cows are seen demurely walking through the forest-paths by the coffee-plantations, and English terriers and pug-dogs sit on the laps of Brazilian ladies. Whether the Jersey cattle will multiply on the planters' estates time will show; but the spread of our colonizing animals, which are now invading simultaneously the plains of Patagonia and the North Canadian territory, does not limit its progress to the direction of the Poles. In India the English horse becomes a colonist by second intention, in the form of the 'Waler.' His value, as compared with the native breeds of Asia, is still undetermined, but we must accept his presence and survival as a fact.

Close on the heels of the purely useful British domesticated animals follow those carried across seas and deserts from motives of sentiment and love of sport. Every week brings news of fresh and successful enterprises of this kind. In Connecticut the beginnings of a most anti-republican system of game-preserving are seen in the success with which pheasants are now being reared. The Connecticut woods are being stocked with these birds, and the State Legislature has passed an Act protecting them for three years. In Texas, according to the *American Field*, there is a Texas State pheasantry, and, in addition, private pheasant-rearing establishments are being opened, 'with a view to the firm establishment of the pheasant as an American game-bird.'

Fish are usually the last British creatures to be established in new countries; the means of transport of the ova is a comparatively modern discovery. But a 'new country' must be already in process of becoming an old one if such a contemplative pursuit as fishing is desired. The most recent 'State-aided migration' of English fish has been to Cape Colony. There Mr. E. Latour has been engaged since 1892 in hatching out *salmo fario*, Loch Leven trout, and brook-trout for stocking the Buffalo River and other South African streams. The work was begun at a large brewery, the cool spring which suited the manufacture of British beer being also adapted for the British fish. Later the work was carried on with great success at the hatchery of the King William's Town Acclimatization Society, six hundred miles from Cape Town. The eggs mainly came from Guildford and Haslemere, and hatched well, tens of thousands of fry being reared. The only doubt is whether the fish which can live as fry in the cool upper waters of these rivers will endure the higher temperature of the lower reaches.

VIII.—IRISH DONKEYS FOR SOUTH AFRICA

THE *St. James's Gazette* thinks that there is a brilliant future before the Irish donkey. He is the future beast of burden of South Africa, where he defies the tsetse-fly in some districts, and is everywhere proof against the climate. English and Dutch dealers have been buying thousands of them for shipment to South Africa, and £5,000 has recently been spent in this way in Clare, Limerick and Tipperary alone.

Ireland is at present the main home of the donkey in the British Islands. Two hundred thousand are annually thence exported to England. They are small, stunted animals, with plenty of endurance, which the donkey never loses, but showing all the worst results of neglect in breeding. As this is the only domestic animal which we have neglected to improve, the results are useful as a scientific example of what happens when domestic animals are 'left to themselves.' Improved animals—sheep, cattle, or horses, down to cats—are full of 'excellent differences.' Our neglected donkeys, never 'bred for points,' have sunk to a dead and dull uniformity of colour, size, shape and even of demeanour.* How different from the gay thirteen-hand 'station' donkey whom your English host puts at your disposal at Ramleh. He meets you at the station, starts off at full gallop, rushes in at the home-gate, and pulls up unasked at the mounting-block by the house. Next day he meets you there, gallops off to the station, and pulls up at a mounting-block of the same kind under the veranda. Authority states the reign of Elizabeth as the period at which the use of donkeys first became general in England. The fact was observed then, but their introduction was, we imagine, due to the connection with Spain, established in the reign of Queen Mary. The Spanish ladies and Spanish priests who visited the Court brought with them their fine donkeys and mules, the proper animals for ladies and ecclesiastics to ride or drive. When the social ascendancy of Spanish fashions ended with the accession of Elizabeth, the rigid social lines drawn between the life of men, ladies and ecclesiastics in Spain, and temporarily introduced here, were broken down. One side-feature of this social revolution, and the elimination of what was

* In Norfolk, where some attention is paid to breeding donkeys, it is noticeable that their colour varies considerably, and an average Norfolk donkey stands quite a hand higher than most of those seen in London.

almost a sumptuary law, was the advance of the horse to the first place for the use of all three 'estates,' lords, ladies, and bishops, and the total eclipse of the ass. The fine animals kept for the purpose of breeding mules were only mated with other donkeys, for mule-breeding ceased. In the pictures of the procession of the Field of the Cloth of Gold, Cardinal Wolsey rides on a mule beside his King. Our donkeys have never recovered from the social results of the Reformation. From that time till the end of the last century the black-coated, full-wigged ecclesiastic on his cob figures in all pictures of equestrian gatherings and State functions, from the caricatures of Bunbury to the Court processions of the Georges. Spenser, with intentional archaism, represents Una riding beside the red-cross knight on a white ass. It is the last poetical tribute to the donkey paid in the Tudor period, and is more than counterbalanced by the part he plays in *Midsummer Night's Dream*. No one who reads the metamorphosis of Bottom can deny that Shakespeare makes a 'true generalization of character' in this study of the true inwardness of donkeys, and that the poor man's animal of that time must have been already much the same as he is now. There must have been plenty of good male donkeys in the country for mule-breeding, but the stock has never been replenished or improved. They have steadily dwindled in size until they have reached the limit set by bad food, want of shelter, and neglect in selection, in the tiny, half-wild donkeys of the New Forest. The sole luxury in life which the New Forest donkey enjoys is the privilege of rolling in the dust on the fenceless roads on a hot day. Yet he is not ill-tempered, and will draw a forest cart with a couple of women in it at a trot for four or five miles very comfortably. In Wales the small tenants do improve their donkeys by giving them better food than common, and often make a high price for them. Both in Somersetshire, near the coal measures, and in Norfolk, by the coast, the animals are in request, and are recognised as a useful help to the poor man; but they are as far removed from the prize sixteen-hand animal of Kentucky agricultural shows as the Shetland pony is from the Shire horse. Donkeys are just the kind of animals which the peasant-proprietor finds useful. A proof of it is seen in the number already reared in Ireland and the surplus available for export. But a little organization and intelligent direction would increase the size and double the value of the breed. The means by which general improvements of this kind are effected are quite familiar from previous experience. If a twentieth part of the pains taken to improve the stock of Irish horses, disclosed in the recent Commission on Irish Horse-breeding, were taken to improve the race of Irish donkeys, the peasant-farmer would have a 'second string' available, most valuable whenever a war or pestilence caused a demand for other than the ordinary transport animals.

The needs of South Africa which have sent buyers to Ireland are exceptional, and unlikely to recur on such a scale. The rinderpest has destroyed the ox transports, and scarcity of grain has starved the horses. But there are two factors which may always be relied on to make a good donkey worth a good price in Rhodesia. These are 'horse sickness' and the tsetse-fly. The astonishing constitution of the donkey makes him less liable to the first, and usually proof against the last of these pests of the new country. As a beast for army transport the donkey is not a mere 'emergency' animal. 'The establishment of breeding-studs, and the greater employment of the donkey as a transport animal, is well worthy of the attention of the military authorities,' writes Major Leonard, after sixteen years' experience as a transport officer. He finds that, used as a pack animal, the smallest donkey will carry an average weight of a hundred and thirty pounds, and the larger ones a hundred and fifty pounds. It can be taken through deserts for journeys of from fifty to sixty hours without water, and pick up food on the way. It has no nerves, and therefore is a first-class animal to take ammunition-boxes to the fighting line. It is small, and less likely to be hit by bullets than a horse, and gets over more difficult ground with less leading. One man can drive ten donkeys on the march, and they need little rations, grooming, or protection from cold.

This being the case for the donkey as he is, it is worth while considering the value of the donkey as he might be. We must assume that under no circumstances will the ass ever bring money 'for show' or fashion, and that none of the increment which improvers of nearly all breeds of high-class animals may expect from this source may be expected in this case. Solid merit will be the only measure of value. This must be obtained by first forming a clear idea of what the different breeds of donkey are capable of doing, and how far they will suit the wants of particular classes. In Syria, where the animal is at its best, there are four breeds of donkey used for work as distinct as that of the different classes of English horse. There are a large rough donkey, standing thirteen and a half hands high, for drawing carts; a heavier kind, used on the farms; a 'gentleman's' riding donkey, standing as high as fourteen hands, comfortable to ride and quick; and a lighter class used for ladies. No one in this country would ride a donkey, except children. His place is in minor traffic here, and for transport by means of packs if exported. The object of the breeder should be to level up the animals all round, just as the standard of Irish cattle has been raised all round.

If anything practical is done in this matter, it will come from above, not from the peasants. If the Dublin Agricultural Society, whose splendid Horse Show and fine buildings are one of the best institutions of the kind in the United Kingdom, could be induced to interest themselves, the movement would have the best chance of success. It might be considered *infra dig.* to include donkeys in the show, but that is only a question of custom, and of the quality of the animals exhibited. In the great agricultural shows of Kentucky one day is always reserved for judging donkeys, and the price of a thousand pounds has been paid for a donkey sire.

IX.—SHIRE HORSES AT ISLINGTON

THE Londoner's comment on the 'English elephants' shown at the Agricultural Hall is that they are 'all alike.' So they are in general form and appearance; and as, unlike the distinct and varied breeds of pedigree cattle, they are all intended for the same purpose, the result is a triumph for those who, since the Shire Horse Society was formed, have spent time and money in producing them.

The total number exhibited has risen to five hundred and fifty-three. In 1880, when the show was first held, it was one hundred and sixty-five, and the increase of numbers shown is a measure of the rise and growth of the latest of the great English industries of breeding pedigree stock, for which this century has been so remarkable. The show, though the entries are so large, is not impressive as a spectacle. All the stallions are shut up in high loose-boxes, and can only be visited separately. The mares are in stalls, and though both are in high condition, the back views so obtained suggest little but the fact of enormous propulsive powers, and the use of a pair of steps for getting on their backs. When alongside them in the stalls and boxes, the impression of bulk is equally great, and the meekness with which they 'get over' when smacked is almost as surprising as the obedience of an elephant. When taken out some new discovery has dictated that their backs and loins shall be thickly covered with sawdust to prevent their catching cold. Consequently a group of a dozen in the ring suggest recollections of magnums of tawny port in a wine-merchant's window. As an unconventional index of their size, the following figures, taken from the measurements of a prize mare and prize stallion, are somewhat interesting. Feet and inches give a clearer idea of dimensions to most minds, so we substitute them for hands. Taking the lady shire horse first, we find that she measures 5 feet 6 inches at the shoulder, 8 inches across the hollow of her front foot, 8 feet 2 inches—98 inches—round her 'waist.' She weighs $18\frac{1}{2}$ cwt. and is not fat. Her 'hair,' which is 5 feet long, is plaited, so that its beauties do not show; but her complexion, dappled brown and glossy, is perfection.

At the other end of the hall a prize stallion, ten years old, and therefore fully mature, was measured with the following results: Height at the shoulder, 5 feet 8 inches, with a 'waist' measurement of

8½ feet; his weight, 1 ton 1½ cwt. His shoe measured 21 inches round from heel to heel, to which the space between the calkins must be added. The stallion's height sometimes runs to 18 hands, and a mane 6 feet long is not uncommon. The average shire horse begins work in the country at four years old, and at five and a half years old goes to town, where two do the work of three ordinary draught-horses, and save the cost of stabling for one. The pedigrees of 16,480 stallions and 22,768 mares are recorded in the 'Shire Horse Stud Book.' This is not a mere catalogue, but has a practical object. Though 'like breeds like,' it is found by experience that the animals of oldest descent, when a breed is once established, produce the most uniform stock. This rule is what the foreign buyer relies on, and it is the world outside England on whom our breeders mainly rely to make the demand for our shire horses keep pace with the supply. Ten years ago three hundred foals were bought for Germany, six hundred 'certificates' of exported sires were issued for America, and it was in evidence that *many hundreds* of farmers in the worst times of the agricultural depression paid their rents from the produce of pedigree mares working on their farms. Since then the demand has risen by leaps and bounds, and the value of the animals has steadily increased. In no long time the prices must fall, because the number of pedigree animals will be beyond measure increased. But the financial result, spread over a wider field, will be even more satisfactory than at present, just as the broad improvement of shorthorn cattle has added to the wealth not of individuals, but of the country—it has raised the value of Irish exported cattle, for instance, by some three pounds per head. At present the prices for shire horses are steadily rising, both for actual work and for breeding. Mr. Freeman Mitford, President of the Society, obtained seven hundred and twenty guineas for a six-year-old stallion, three hundred and twenty guineas for a three-year-old mare, and two hundred and ten guineas for a yearling filly.

At Lord Wantage's sale no less than eight hundred guineas was paid for a six-year-old mare. Messrs. Clark and Griffin, farmers, were as successful in a recent sale as their wealthier competitors, making an average of £150 for their shire horses. The 'man in the street' would scarcely believe that the big, slow horses in the railway-van are often more valuable than the showy animals in the landau which passes them; but this is often the case, and the former justify their price by work done. In developing the size of these horses, only one serious drawback has been encountered by the breeders. Their enormous weight causes a tendency to an ossification of the side cartilage of the foot, which is called 'side-bone.'

One of the main objects of the Shire Horse Society is to 'breed away from side-bone,' and it is to their success in this that the popularity of the breed is largely due. Hence the importance of pedigree, and incidentally the delay in awarding prizes in the show; for every animal has to pass a rigorous 'medical examination' before its merits are considered. A second, and not less important, form of soundness in these animals is temper. 'Temperament' is perhaps the truer word. In combining this mental characteristic with modifications in size and strength, the breeders have met with little resistance from Nature. If the 'nerves' of the ordinary thoroughbred or hackney were possessed by the giant shire horse, it would be as unsafe to use for traffic as a Highland bull, and almost as dangerous as a stampeding elephant. If its nerves did not occasionally cause it to bolt with a two-ton van behind it, the everyday fidgeting, stamping and trotting which ordinary equine temperament demands in the lighter horses would strain the legs and ruin the hoofs which have to bear the burden of its bulk. As things are, the temper of the great horse has grown milder and easier as its size has increased. This is largely due to nature, for the shire horse is descended, without Arab or thoroughbred crosses, from the heavy war-horse of the days of armour. But the avoidance of repeating any cross from which temper has resulted must also be credited to the breeders' experience. The nature of the shire horse's work does not ordinarily disturb this innate equanimity. They are never urged to speed. On the other hand, they are constantly required to make sudden exertions in pulling and hauling great weights, exertions which require as much resolution on the part of the horse, and urging by the 'driver,' as efforts of speed. Yet the shire horse works entirely by the voice. He is never struck with the whip; a hand on the reins by his mouth, a friendly pull, and a word or two, are enough to make him exert a muscular power greater than that of any other domesticated animal but the elephant. This docility has been acquired without loss of courage or intelligence. Men who have been employed for twenty years in superintending the shire horse at work say that he never knows when he is beaten. The most trying work he is employed in is that of carting earth from excavations, or loads of stone and material to line cuttings and reservoirs. To do so he draws his loads, not over roads of macadam or stone, but over yielding earth or clay. The load has usually to be started up an incline, yet the horse obeys orders, and will renew the effort again and again at the word of command. The camel, which often refuses to move if overloaded, is perhaps wiser in its generation. The intelligence of the shire horse is not only not less, but greater, than that of most breeds. This is partly due to its constant association with its carter in work other than mere monotonous driving. The cleverness of the shire horses on the railway is matter of common observation. But the quiet wits of the contractors' horses are less well known. An instance, noticed while a new reservoir was being dug above the grounds of the Ranelagh Club, gives some idea of the intelligence which 'informs' these colossal horses. Heavy loads of earth from an excavation were being raised in a 'hopper' and dropped into a 'tipping-cart.' This was run violently along some rough rails, and at the last moment a pin was loosened, and the earth shot over the end of the embankment. Instead of being *pushed* by an engine, the cart was pulled, at the highest speed that could be raised, by a young shire horse. To 'work the machine,' it had first to start the cart full of earth, to rush it along at a half-trot, half-canter, and at the last moment to jump on one side off the line, to have its hauling-chain detached by an automatic slip jerked by the driver, and to let the one and a quarter tons of earth and the truck rush past it and bang against the chocks at the end of the rail, spilling the earth from the hopper. If he failed to spring aside at the last moment, he would be jammed between the trolly and the blocks, or thrown over the slope of the embankment. The side-spring had to be made when going fast and using great exertion. The horse was very excited, but never 'lost its head,' or showed the least inclination to shirk the work. Its driver, or rather attendant, had taught it to do this in *four days*, and the horse, though very large, was only a four-year-old. But Lord Herbert of Cherbury wrote the character of the 'great horse' of England more than two hundred years ago, and noted that he was a creature 'made above all others for the service of man.' Among other accomplishments, he taught him to run at a figure dressed in bright armour, and knock it over 'in the midst of a field.'

X.—THE BEAUTY OF CATTLE

A VISIT to the Cattle Show at the Agricultural Hall should reconcile the English mind to the Indian worship of the cow. Considered as a gathering of the most beautiful animals of their kind which the art of man can aid Nature to produce, it has only one drawback—the excess of flesh which a 'fat-stock' show demands. But the richness and colour of the cattle, and the noble lines of heads, dark-eyed and massive-browed, with curling locks upon their foreheads and shining crescent horns, make a study of form and colour which the most uninstructed sight-seer must admire. Our impression of the show, from the point of view of the animals' comfort or suffering, was, on the whole, favourable. The atmosphere was beautifully sweet and clean, with a pleasant smell of hay and clover and clean straw —scents that must suggest to the cattle's mind visions of a glorified rickyard. It is, perhaps, too hot for the comfort of the fatter beasts, some of whom pant and show signs of *malaise*. But others were lying down and chewing the cud placidly, or licking their own coats or those of their neighbours—attentions to toilet which are a certain sign of contentment in cattle. The least tranquil was the splendid steer which had won the highest honours of the show. Size, shape, and colour would have qualified it for a place among the Oxen of the Sun. Almost as tall as an Indian bison, with a back as straight and level as a table, it had the characteristic colour and proportions of the finest domestic breed. The blue-roan mottling of its wavy coat gradually increased in closeness, until on its neck and head nothing but the dark tint, like 'blued' steel, prevailed. Its eyes were large and black, its eyelashes long and curling, its muzzle fine and sensitive. But its whole aspect was melancholy, as it waved its head wearily from side to side. As we watched it, it lay down, for the first time since entering the show, and before long was no doubt reconciled to its surroundings. This steer weighed 1 ton 1 cwt., and was barely three and a half years old. But the weariness of the champion was by no means shared by its fellows. A lovely steer from Norwich, next door, was dipping its nose alternately into its water-pail and supper-tray; and a beautiful young blue-gray bullock, from Lord Ellesmere's park near Newmarket, was angrily protesting at being kept waiting while his neighbours were fed. His groom, a bright Suffolk lad who had 'known him ever since he was a baby,' treated this young giant as if he were a Newfoundland dog. 'Come, kiss me, then,' he said, pulling the halter, as his pet was busy munching bran and turnips, and the animal actually raised its bran-covered muzzle from the tray to give the required salute. The 'cross-breds'—cattle produced from parents of first-class merit, but of different stocks—are always the most interesting class in the show. There is no saying what new beauties may be produced from the mating of the finest specimens of different pure-bred cattle. The champion of the show was the son of a shorthorn bull and a Galloway cow; in others of almost equal merit the strain of Suffolk, or Devon, or Welsh blood was to be traced. Great variety of colour results from this mixture of strains; black, blue-roan, iron-gray, and deep chestnut-red being the favourite tints. These long-haired, richly-tinted hides should make admirable rugs for halls. The Herefords are, perhaps, the most distinct in appearance of any breed, except the Highlanders. Their coats are crisp and curly, their bodies a rich, deep red, and the face pure white, with a white line up the nape of the neck. Very different to these easy-going English cattle are the wild Highlanders tethered opposite. Purity of blood only brings out their Celtic constitution in the greatest perfection. Their shaggy coats hang in mops and elf-locks over their eyes, and their eyes are restless and

Rob Roy's Cattle.

angry. Some have enormous horns, bent like the bow of Ulysses; in others, one horn curls up and the other down, lending a disreputable jauntiness to their unkempt heads. Some are orange-yellow; others the colour of old dead wood or smoky glass. Others are tawny and shaggy like a water-spaniel. Even the railway journey and the show does not subdue their irascible Celtic minds; and one rugged Highlander, after being hauled in by a dozen reluctant drovers, was, in order to secure peace, blindfolded with a sack, beneath which he sulked like a Skye-terrier in disgrace. No greater contrast could be imagined than that presented by these lineal descendants of the great *bos urus* of the Caledonian forest, and the placid, silky-coated shorthorns, the latest triumphs of domestication. The prize shorthorn heifer was, perhaps, the ideal of a nice, good-tempered 'cushy' cow. The white coat shone like ivory satin on her back; her black eyes and eyelashes set off her shapely head; her ears just brushed her pink horns, and her forehead was starred with little velvet curls. The neat, white, cotton-plaited headstall which confined her did not prevent her pushing her muzzle into every extended hand to seek for food, and she tossed her head, when they were without a gift, in the keenest disappointment and mortification. Compared with her, the tiny black Kerry cows looked mere pigmies. Yet their form was equally perfect, and their quick vivacious movements proclaimed their race as clearly as their robbery of their neighbours' hay showed their hereditary capacity for taking care of themselves in good times or in bad. These small Kerry cows are perhaps the best cattle which can be kept in the grounds of a moderate country house. They are too small to damage fences, are capital milkers, and most affectionate and intelligent pets. They are naturally friendly creatures, and, like cows in general, have, perhaps, longer memories for people than any other animal. For the farm, the choice will naturally fall among the larger breeds. The difficulty must be, not to choose well where all are so good, but to make a choice at all. In addition to the specific breeds we have mentioned, there are towering black Welsh cattle, curly and horned; and the deep-red steers of Sussex, small and compact, with crescent horns; black, polled Galloways, with coats shining like astrachan wool; and lovely Devons, redder than their native marl, and matched in colour to a hair. These are the herds that have stocked the ranches of the Argentine and the runs of New South Wales, the hills of New Zealand, and the plains of Uruguay. It is for their protection that the breeder demands a check on the importation of cattle diseases from abroad; and the Cattle Show is the most convincing argument which his cause has yet produced.

The naturalist who is not too proud to know the

history of the domesticated animals which are now as native to the soil as any of the ancient wild races could name any district in which he found himself by a glance at the sheep upon the hills. Not even the cattle exhibit such marked differences as are to be found in the flocks which a century of careful selection has fitted to thrive best in the varied soils of England. The big Leicester sheep, with long gray wool and white faces, are as different from the 'Cotswolds' as a Newfoundland from a white poodle. In the 'Cotswolds' will be found the original of the 'baa-lamb' of the nursery. These sheep are tall, with *white* wool in locks, and with tufts upon the head and forehead. The Lincolnshire sheep are more like those of Leicester, but heavier in the fleece, coarser, and more fitted for life in the marshes. They have, perhaps, the most intelligent faces of any sheep but the refined South Downs. We noticed a Lincoln ewe endeavouring to open a sack of cakes by putting her foot into the mouth, and drawing out the contents, as it lay on the ground in the next pen. Romney Marsh has its own breed of sheep, somewhat like the Lincolns. But of all the flocks of England, the South Downs must win the palm. Their short-clipped and delicate wool is felted together like moss. The hand sinks into it with difficulty. The form is beautiful and rounded, and though apparently so finely built, their weight is great.

The close, yellow-gray fleece fits over the head like a cap, disclosing the face and nose, covered with short, gray hair—not wool. The features are extremely dainty, and the movements of the mouth, as the sheep nibbles its fragrant supper of trefoil and clover, resemble those of some delicate foreign rodent. Their heads are far prettier than those of many deer—almost as refined as that of the gazelle. These sheep undergo an elaborate toilet every morning. Clipping them is an art in which few excel. Their coats are trimmed, brushed, and damped, and pressed flat with a setting-board, and finally tinted for the day. The Hampshires, black-faced and Roman-nosed, are also rouged.

It would be interesting to trace the development of these fine creatures from their primitive ancestors; but even in the earliest instance the sheep seems not to have been indigenous in England. Geologically speaking, it is a very modern animal. Oddly enough, the chief difference between the tame and the wild sheep seems to be in the length of its tail, which is short in all the wild breeds, and *will* grow long in domesticated sheep, though severely discouraged in this country. The wool in the tame sheep has also gained that power of 'felting' on which its value mainly depends. The wild cattle of Chillingham are this year not represented at the Show. The animal shown last year, which was the result of a cross with a pure-bred shorthorn, retained the characteristic colour and shape of the original herd, even in the horns and tip of the ear, a proof of the strength of the wild blood which has been observed in several previous experiments. It took a good place among the best cross-breds exhibited, and made excellent beef when killed.

Swine have probably made the widest departure from the wild state. A bird's-eye view of the piggery, taken from the top of a corn-bin, showed nothing but round and placid-breathing masses of animated pork, shapeless and unpleasing, excellent, no doubt, for food; but how unlike the old rusty-coloured, vivacious, sagacious English woodland pig! Professor Flower says that the young of all wild kinds of pig present a uniform coloration, being dark brown with longitudinal stripes of a paler colour. This marking, according to our own observation, is very rare in the domesticated pig, which seems to have lost with civilization all distinguishing marks of its wild parentage. It would be a pity, however, if the poor piggies at Islington were made into 'burnt pig,' after the manner invented by Charles Lamb's Chinaman. That, however, may well be the case unless the rules against smoking in the Cattle Show are more strictly enforced. We saw one visitor knock the ashes off his cigar into a pen. A fire so kindled might run the length of the hall in ten minutes, and not leave a single beast surviving.

XI.—WAR-HORSES

WAR and the chase are the ultimate objects for which the Commission on Irish Horse-breeding has lately been hearing the evidence of experts on both sides of the Channel. The Irish owners desire to raise a class of horses the best of which can be sold at a high price for hunting, while the rest pay their way as cavalry remounts. How best to combine these objects the Commission will have to decide. Thoroughbred sires, it is agreed, produce the stock most likely to make good hunters; and though the 'hackney' is much in favour with some breeders of cavalry horses, we have very little doubt that the better bred these are the more likely they are to stand the rough work of war.

The modern heavy cavalry horse has to carry a total weight, made up of man, harness, and equipment, of 20 st.—280 lb.—and the light cavalry horse a weight of 17 st. He is expected, if required, to march thirty miles in one day, and to be able to do his work on the next. Bought in Ireland at three years old, he is two years in training, and spends four years in the ranks as his average time of active service. It is very possible that if the type of cavalry horse were bigger it would last longer. But the modern animal is a compromise between the needs of the Service and the price which Government can afford. There is no such contrast now as formerly between the great war-horse, specially bred to carry the man in armour, and the 'natural' war-horse, bred for speed, endurance, and to carry a man armed only with sword, spear, and shield. The difference has never been presented so vividly as in the battles of the Crusaders, especially those in which they were opposed to the Saracen cavalry. Sir Walter Scott's representation of the single combat in the desert between Sir Kenneth and Saladin is a very probable account of what would happen in such an encounter. When the mail-clad Knights on their heavy horses were able to charge knee to knee they must have swept away any force of Saracen cavalry; but there is evidence in the accounts of the Templars that they modified their equipment in some degree to suit the Eastern modes of warfare and the climate. It is, however, less well known that the Saracens did the same, and that the changes they made in the days of the Crusades endured a hundred years ago, and in some parts of the Soudan are still observable. They adopted a light chain armour, the steel cap, and the two-handed sword of the

Crusaders, and to carry the increased weight must have bred their horses of a larger size. This appears in an account by Bruce in his 'Travels to Discover the Source of the Nile,' published exactly one hundred years ago. He visited, near Sennaar, the Sheik Adelan, round whose house were stabled four hundred horses, with quarters for four hundred men, all alike the 'property' of Sheik Adelan. 'It was one of the finest sights I ever saw of the kind,' he wrote. 'The horses were all above sixteen hands high, of the breed of the old Saracen horses, all finely made and as strong as our coach-horses, but exceedingly nimble in their motion; rather thick and short in the fore-hand, but with the most beautiful eyes, ears, and heads in the world. They were mostly black, some of them black and white, some of them milk-white (foaled so, not white by age).' The size and character of these horses distinguish them from the ordinary light Arab. Sir William Broadwood questions Bruce's accuracy, saying that he is evidently mistaken when he describes Sheik Adelan's troop-horses as all above sixteen hands, because Arab horses now rarely exceed fifteen hands. Bruce's accuracy has survived the questioning of his contemporary critics, but the context supplies a probable answer to Sir W. Broadwood's doubts. All the riders wore armour, and the horses were not the modern Arab, but bred to carry the extra weight. 'A steel shirt of mail hung over each man's quarters opposite his horse, and by it an antelope's skin, made as soft as chamois, with which it was covered from the dew of night. A headpiece of copper, without crest or plume, was suspended by a lace above this shirt of mail, and was the most picturesque part of the trophy. To these was added an enormous broadsword, in a red leather scabbard, and upon the pommel hung two thick gloves, like hedger's gloves, their fingers in one poke.' To carry this panoply the Sheik's horses were modified from the natural Arab type.

The size of the English war-horse reached its maximum in the reign of Henry VIII., when the relations of body-armour to 'hand-guns' were analogous to those of the early ship-armour and cannon before the 'high velocities' were obtained at Elswick. There was good reason to believe that by adding a little to the thickness of the coat of steel the soft low-velocity bullet of the day could be kept out. So it was for a time. But the additional weight required a still larger horse to carry it. The charger had to be armoured as well as his rider, and the collection in the Tower of London shows the actual weight which it carried. The panoply of Charles Brandon, Duke of Suffolk, the brother-in-law of Henry VIII., still exists. That of the horse covers the whole of the hind-quarters, the back of the neck, forehead, muzzle, ears, shoulders, and chest. It is exactly like a piece of boiler-plating, and fastened by rivets. The rider sat in a saddle the front of which was a steel shield ten inches high, covering the stomach and thighs as the 'breast-work' on an ironclad's deck covers the base of the turret. The total weight is 80 lb. 15 oz. To this add the weight of the rider's armour, 99 lb. 9 oz., and of the rider himself, say, 16 st.—224 lb.—and the total is 28 st. 12 lb. 8 oz., or 404 lb. 8 oz. This bears out Holinshed's statement that in the days of Henry VIII., 'who erected a noble studderie for breeding horses, especially the greatest sort,' such as were kept for burden, would bear 4 cwt. commonly. As the gun prevailed, personal armour, just as in the modern ships, was concentrated over the vital parts. Breastplates remained bullet-proof, thigh-pieces were only sword-proof. But till the days of James II. *complete* armour seems to have been commonly worn by commanding officers in battle. The statue of Admiral Lord Holmes in Yarmouth Church shows him in full armour. Charles I., Cromwell, Maurice of Nassau, and William III. at the Boyne, are painted in the same equipment, except that leather boots have superseded greaves. The horse becomes lighter, but is in most respects the same animal. His points are well shown in the fine equestrian statue of Charles II. at the top of Whitehall Place. But before the date of the battle of Blenheim a change had begun. The 'great horse' of war was being bred as a beast of draught, to develop into the modern shire horse, and his place as a war-horse was in process of being taken by the 'dragooner,' which carried a soldier with only as much defensive armour as our modern Lifeguards. Cromwell's 'dragooners' carried rather more weight; but from a letter quoted by Sir Walter Gilbey in 'The Old English War-Horse,'* it may be inferred that they were not of the old heavy breed. 'Buy those horses,' he writes to Auditor Squire, 'but do not give more than eighteen or twenty pieces each for them. That is enough for dragooners.' Then, 'I will give you sixty pieces for that black you won (in battle) at Horncastle, for my son has a mind to him.' The 'black' was one of the old war-horses, the colour having become synonymous with the breed; and Oliver was so keen on getting it, that as Mr. Auditor Squire would not part at the price offered, he wrote later: 'I will give you all you ask for that black you won last fight.' By the accession of the Hanoverian Kings the 'great horse' had disappeared, even for the use of officers and commanders. Then the equipment of regular cavalry became uniform throughout the whole of Europe, and has remained so until the present day. The only difference in the horses is that between an animal able

* 'The Old English War-Horse.' By Walter Gilbey. London: Vinton and Co.

to carry a 12 st. man and his equipment, and that which carries a 10 st. man, and except in some French regiments of Chasseurs which use Arab horses, the breed is almost identical. Even the Cossacks are now regular troopers and mounted on big horses, instead of the twelve-hand ponies on which they rode from the Don to the Seine.

In the Græco-Turkish War the Greek army encamped on the plain where Bucephalus was reared; but the famous Thessalian horses have now dwindled to the size of ponies, which were ridden by the irregular and local levies of the Greeks. Bucephalus was the most costly war-horse ever bought. The animal came out of a noted stud owned by a Thessalian chief; and even before its celebrated taming by Alexander, this gentleman asked Philip £2,518 15s. as his lowest price. Pliny says that Philip gave £435 more than this. It now appears that, contrary to general belief, Bucephalus was a *mare*. This accounts for the high price paid. Compared with the prices asked for Arab mares of great descent in much later times, the sum demanded is not excessive. But Bucephalus was a good bargain even as a war-horse. She was ridden until she was thirty years old, and then died of wounds received in a battle with Porus, and left her bones in the Punjab.

XII.—THE SPEED OF THE PIGEON-POST

It seems probable that current estimates of the speed of birds' flight must be modified. In a recent race a number of carrier-pigeons were flown from the Shetland Islands to London. This is a great distance even for trained birds, the total length of the journey being 591½ miles. The date being only a week after the longest day of the year, the birds had the advantage of daylight during their whole flight, and the winner reached the house of its owner, Mr. Clutterbuck, of Stanmore, in eight minutes under sixteen hours. They had been liberated at Lerwick at 3.30 a.m. The official weather-chart of the Meteorological Office gave, not for the first time, information of the utmost value for estimating the conditions of wind under which the flight was made. Every 'arrow' from Kirkwall to London pointed due south. In other words, the birds had the wind behind them throughout their journey. The result is that, in what is very nearly an approach to a migration flight, the pigeons travelled at a speed of

37 miles an hour. An interesting correspondence in the *Field*, following the announcement of this fact, showed how widely observers differ on this most interesting question, but the records approach more nearly to the lower estimate in each case in which accuracy has been possible ; and in any case the surmises of the late Dr. Gätke that migrating birds travelled occasionally at speeds reaching 180 miles an hour cannot now be seriously defended. Yet such a good observer as Mr. Frohawk, one of our best painters of birds and animals, is convinced that a godwit can fly at a speed ot 150 miles per hour ; and Sir Ralph Payne Gallwey reckons the flight of a teal as sometimes reaching 140 miles an hour. But it has been calculated that if the godwit were flying at 150 miles an hour, it would have to overcome a resistance of air equal to a pressure of 112 lb. per square foot, or considerably more than the force of a hundred-mile hurricane. Other correspondents give instances which leave little doubt that shore birds do travel at speeds considerably above 50 miles an hour ; but as regards the flight of the pigeon, some experiments carried out by the proprietors of the *Field* many years ago leave little doubt that the speed shown in the Shetland flight is normal. Twelve records with the chronograph gave a highest speed to the 'blue rock' pigeon of from 33 to 38 miles an hour. Pheasants and partridges were also subjected to

experiment. The former made a record of 38 miles an hour, and the partridges, when well on the wing, of 32 miles.

The correspondents of the *Field* have endeavoured to settle the question of the speed of birds solely by observation. In the absence of any mechanical aids such observations are most difficult to make, and in the nature of things they fall short of the certainty which would be desirable. The chief value of such contributions to the discussion is that up to the present date first-hand observations of any kind are scarce, meagre, and contradictory. Everyone has been struck by the phenomena of flight; almost no one has found time to take the necessary thought and trouble to collect data on a subject so uncertain and elusive. When M. Marey published his monumental work, 'Le Vol des Oiseaux,' in 1890, such records as he was able to collect, though eminently suggestive, were only calculated to give uncertain notions; moreover, the conclusions of different writers did not agree. M. Van Roosebeck, a leading Belgian pigeon-flyer, assigned to homing pigeons a maximum speed of from 100 to 120 miles an hour. Wilbers quoted a case of a pigeon which had flown nearly 20 miles in as many minutes. Here is a difference of one half between two authorities. One of the standard references was an observed flight of pigeons from Paris to Spa, at the rate of 50 miles an hour.

The distance between the two points is 250 miles. Some of the so-called tables of birds' speed must have been drawn up on pure conjecture. Thus, according to one authority, the quail flies at 17 metres per second, the pigeon at 27 metres, the falcon at 28 metres (what falcon?), the swallow at 67 metres, and the martin at 88 metres, or about 95 yards per second. Such comparisons are useless without stating what kind of flight is meant. The only flight which is open to comparison in the sense desired, or rather which can be compared with the means at our disposal, is the sustained flight of birds from point to point. Not, for example, the downward rush of a falcon after prey, or the dash of a partridge into cover. But there are cases in which even these can be compared, as when a bird of prey pursues another bird. In this connection this table of speeds is ridiculously inaccurate; the writer has seen a small falcon, the hobby, pursue and catch a swallow on the wing, though the speed of the latter is set down as four times greater than that of the falcon. Audubon's notes are more interesting, and probably nearer the truth. He found in the crops of pigeons which he shot some rice, which they could not have gathered nearer than Carolina, about 350 miles from the place where they were shot. From the state of digestion in which he found the rice, he concluded that it had been six hours in the birds' crops, and that they must therefore have flown the distance at a speed of about a mile a minute. He also estimated that the eider-duck flies at the speed of 40 miles an hour, and the wild duck at about 45 miles an hour in sustained flights. One obvious chance of error in his calculation of the speed of the pigeons is the possibility that digestion may have been partly arrested while the birds were flying so long a distance. Another statement dealing with the frigate-bird depends on the assumption that it neither flies by night nor sleeps on the water. If this is correct, the distances travelled by these ocean-birds in a single day must amount to as much as 1,800 miles, for they have been seen at a distance of more than 900 miles from any coast or island. But no one can prove that they do not fly by night, and the effortless soaring of these ocean-birds suggests that their power to remain on the wing is certainly not limited to a period of twelve hours.

It seems contrary to all reasonable conjecture that any bird should make a daily flight of hundreds of miles from its roosting-place. But there are means available for discovering the real rate of flight of the frigate-bird not less accurately than that of the carrier-pigeon. According to the Rev. S. G. Whitmee, the frigate-birds are domesticated by the natives of the Ellice Islands. In 1870 he saw numbers of them sitting about on perches erected for them near the beach. The natives catch the young birds, tie them by the leg, and feed them till they become tame. Then they let them loose, when they regularly go out to sea to obtain food, and come back to roost. Advantage was taken of this by some of the missionaries to establish a 'pigeon-post,' conducted by frigate-birds, between the islands, and Mr. Whitmee himself saw more than one letter arrive in a quill attached to the wing of a frigate-bird. Here there is a perfect opportunity, ready made, for determining the speed of one of the finest fliers among the whole nation of birds. It is not likely that the natives of these islands, or, rather, islets, north of Fiji and east of Samoa, have ceased to tame the birds, and the missionaries now on the islands might renew the experiment of the past, and make a trustworthy record. A very ingenious means of observing the speed of flight was suggested by MM. Liais and Mouillard. This was to fly a bird across some open area of sand, and measure the time at which the shadow crossed lines marked upon it. But the photographic gun of M. Marey gives excellent results. If the bird is crossing the spectator, it will show on a spinning disc images at the rate of ten in a second. When the space between the images is measured, and compared with the length of the bird's body on the plate, the speed at which it is travelling can be calculated at once. Observations made from railway-carriage windows give a rough means of comparing bird-speed. The writer has often done this, and has found that a train running at thirty-five miles an hour travels faster than the rook, the heron, the pheasant, and all small birds commonly seen inland except swallows and martins. A covey of partridges flying parallel with the train sometimes exceeds the speed of the engine at between thirty-five and forty miles per hour. Accurate observations of the flight of cormorants might be made, if anyone would take the necessary trouble, when returning to roost in the cliffs. They fly perfectly straight along shore in certain places just before dusk every evening, and a few marks set up and a measurement on the ordnance map would give accurate results, especially if two persons marked the flight at different angles. The writer has found the speed of these heavy birds, on still evenings, to approximate to a mile in one minute and ten seconds. 'A mile a minute' is less rapid when the flight is watched from a distance than might be imagined. It must be something less than half the speed at which a swift dashes past on a summer evening, though allowances must be made for appearances when comparing the flight of large birds with that of small ones. A bee seems to fly by like a flash, yet it only makes thirty miles an hour, or half the speed at which the heavy cormorants fly home to bed.

XIII.—THE LONDON HORSE AT HOME

LONDON horses are the result of the completest form of 'urban immigration' known. Probably not thirty of the three hundred thousand which live within the Metropolitan area were born there. Yet such is the natural intelligence of their kind that, after a training lasting not more than eight months, even at the longest, they are as much at home in London streets, and as healthy in London stables, as if they had never known the freedom of a Suffolk strawyard or an Irish hillside. Even in manners and appearance the London horse differs from his country cousin. Even the street-arab detects the latter. 'Hullo, here's a country 'orse; let's take a rise out of him!' was the amiable comment of a street-urchin on seeing a rustic Dobbin which had brought a load of hay into town during the summer droughts munching from its nose-bag outside a Chelsea 'public.'

In 'The Horse World of London,' published by the Religious Tract Society, Mr. W. J. Gordon has given not a sketch, but an exhaustive and brightly written account of the varied lives and work of the animals themselves, and of the organized system of collective ownership which mainly governs the employment and purchase of London horses. There is hardly a page in the book which is not full of facts, mainly new, and always interesting. As we read, the mixed and bewildering equine crowd which pours along the streets in carriages and four-wheeled cabs, tradesmen's carts and parcel-vans, brewers' drays and road-carts, dust-cars and coal-carts, hansoms and hearses, is resolved into classes, nations and callings, destined for separate uses, with reasonable purpose. The immense scale on which horses are now 'jobbed' from large proprietors, and the steady decline of private ownership, is perhaps the most interesting fact, from an economic point of view, on which Mr. Gordon dwells. Tilling, of Peckham, owns a stud of 2,500 of all kinds, and these are hired for work in every part of the kingdom, from the heavy cart-horse to the riding-cob. They are to be found in Sunderland, in Cornwall and at Brighton. They are hired by every class of customer, from the Lord Mayor and Sheriffs to the laundry company. Peak and Frean hire a hundred for their biscuit vans ; a great brewer 'jobs' as many more. Even some of the tram-lines are thus horsed ; so is the Fire Brigade, the Salvage Corps, and now the mounted police. The advantage of these large establishments is plain. If a horse turns out unfit for the use for which it is bought, it can be transferred to another. If unsuited for a smart carriage, it can be hired out to the doctor, and if troublesome, can be put to hard labour for a season in an omnibus, and thence transferred, after a course of discipline, to the luxurious life of private service. This is an old device; but hitherto the transfer could not be made without the sale and repurchase of the animal at a loss, until the horseowner increased his stock to a size which made such change of employment possible. One small owner, the possessor of four or five light 'vanners,' was wont to boast that he had bought a horse for five pounds and sold it for fifty pounds, a story which he never varied when relating it to the present writer. The animal, purchased at an equine 'rubbish' sale, was a confirmed bolter. No sooner was it harnessed than it set off at full gallop, a career which generally ended in a smash, and the immediate resale of the culprit. But the new purchaser, far from trying to check this propensity, resolved, as he said, to 'humour him a bit,' and generously '*lent* him to a fire-engine.' The horse soon found that he was encouraged not only to bolt at starting, but to keep up the pace, and in six months was quite ready either to stand in harness or to start at any speed wished by his driver. Besides the great 'jobbers,' the omnibus companies, the railways, the London vestries, and the large breweries and distilleries own troops and regiments of horses, and the combination of capital and high organization with proper economic management in these great establishments has set a standard of good and humane treatment by which the London horse has greatly benefited. Better and larger stables, good food and litter, and steady work, with regular days of rest, have lengthened the life and improved the physique of the London horse. A good brewer's horse, standing 17·2, was weighed by Mr. Gordon, and tipped the beam at just over the ton. The driver weighed 20 stone 12 lb.! the van, fully loaded, 6 tons 15 cwt., to which must be added the harness, making a total with the driver of nearly 8 tons. Three horses drew the whole; and it was stated that, on the average, three horses now do the work which four did twenty years ago. 'The vans have improved, the roads have improved, and the horses have improved—especially the horses.' We agree with Mr. Gordon in thinking that steady attention to the breeding of draught-horses all over the country has probably increased their size and power, just as it has increased the average size of the thoroughbred. The latter gains one hand in a century. In 1700 he stood, on the average, at 13·2; he now stands 15·3. We might suggest a rough test of the growth of the draught-horse. The shafts of the 'tumbril,' or country two-wheeled farm-cart, have probably been set on at their present height by the tradition of one hundred years in wheelwrights' shops. If compared with the height of the shafts in the 'tumbrils' used for the monster horses of the London vestries, a clue might be gained as to the proportionate increase in the height of the best draught-horses. The main conditions of health for the London horse, when once acclimatized, seem to be the Sunday's rest, and proper care of his feet. Experience only proves the truth of the evidence given by Bianconi, when the whole mail traffic of Ireland was run on his cars. He owned more horses than any man of his time, and declared that he got far more work out of them when he ran them only six days a week than when he ran them seven. Mr. Gordon cites Lord Erskine's speech when introducing a Bill dealing with cruelty to animals: 'Man's dominion is not absolute, but is limited by the obligations of justice and mercy;' and, except in the case of certain unfortunate hackneys, which can be used in carts on week-days, and serve in a cab on Sundays, most owners seem now to recognise both the justice and utility of allowing their horses a Sabbath of rest. Hard work is terribly aggravated by any mischief in the horses' feet, most of the cases of 'cruelty' being due to working them in that condition. The ponderous hoof of the dray-horse crushes down upon iron or sharp stone, and at once drives the object deep into the

foot. Iron nails inflict the worst injuries, and when
'demolitions' are going on, or masses of broken
material are being carted through the streets, drags
and vans are often sent by circuitous routes in order
to avoid the nail-studded roadway. Proper shoeing
is almost as important as daily foot examination
for these bulky horses. 'There is no animal more
carefully shod than a brewer's horse,' writes Mr.
Gordon. 'At Courage's, for instance, no such things
as standard sizes are known. Many have a different
make and shape of shoe on each hoof. The shoe is
always made specially to fit the foot, and these are never
thrown away, but are mended—soled and heeled, in fact
—by having pieces of iron welded into them again and
again. Some of the shoes are steel-faced; some are
barred, the shoe going all round the foot; some have
heels, some toes; some one clip, some two. In fact,
there are almost as many makes of shoes as in a
Northampton shoe-factory.'

Mr. Gordon has a separate and amusing treatise on
nearly every branch of the London horse-world, from
the Queen's 'Creams' to the funeral steed and the
typical cab-horse. His story of the request that King
William IV. would delay hastening to the House to
dissolve Parliament in 1831, in order to give time for
the cream-coloured State horses to have their manes
plaited, and the King's reply, 'Plait the manes! I'll

go in a hackney coach,' is part of the tradition of the Buckingham Palace stables. But the sequel of the indignant coachman swearing at the guard of honour, and having to descend from the box and apologize after conveying his Majesty to the House, gives greater finish to the episode. The funeral horses are State steeds in their way also, and, like the Queen's cream-colours, are foreigners, or of foreign extraction. But the creams are of Hanoverian descent. The 'Black Brigade' are all Flemish, and come to London by way of Rotterdam and Harwich. There are nearly seven hundred in London, and these are mainly the property of one or two large owners. 'The jobmaster is at the back of the burying world.' One of these speaks very pleasantly of his black stud. 'I am not a horsey man,' says the undertaker, 'but I have known this class of horse all my life, and I say they are quite affectionate and good-natured, and seem to know instinctively what you say to them and what you want. One thing, they have an immense amount of self-esteem, and that you have to humour. Of course, I have to choose the horses, and I do not choose the vicious ones. I can tell them by the glance they give as they look round at me.' They are very fanciful as to their company, and if a coloured horse is put in the stalls among them, the blacks at once turn fretful and miserable. Mr. Gordon has a fund of stories and experiences of the sale-rooms, the donkey-mart at Islington, and the export and import trade. In spite of the imports from Poland, Finland, Holland, and even America, and the pony trade with the Baltic, our export of horses enormously exceeds the import in value. A three years' total gives £2,532,000 of exports, as against £804,000 of imports, and the quality and price of English horses rise steadily. The imports do not include those from Ireland, which until recently supplied the entire Belgian Army with remounts, and at present largely fill the ranks of London cab-horses. They fetch on the average about £30 a-piece; and as a new hansom-cab costs £100, the hirer enjoys the temporary use of a capital of £130, and the services of the driver. But the number of cabs steadily decreases, and, from the horses' point of view, this decline is hardly to be deplored.

XIV.—MENAGERIE ANIMALS

TRAVELLING wild-beast shows are still among the most popular entertainments in the world, and, contrary to general opinion, the animals are usually both healthy and happy in these peripatetic companies. The late Mr. A. D. Bartlett stated that in his experience animals of the cat tribe in travelling wild-beast shows far more often had litters of cubs than those kept in the comparative comfort of the Zoological Gardens, and that they were also more healthy, probably on account of the change of air and excitement. But though animals on tour are seldom sick or 'sorry,' experience shows that they must have periods of rest. This is especially the case with the elephants, camels, zebras, and other creatures which not only travel on foot in all weathers during the greater part of the year, but also take part in performances, and often have to aid in drawing heavy caravans. When they arrive at the town where the show is to be exhibited in the evening, they are stabled and fed ; but an afternoon performance, and at least three hours of light, noise, and excitement every evening, though very much enjoyed by the elephants, try their nerves and make quiet necessary. Most of the big wild-beast shows and circuses own a kind of dockyard and hospital, to which both live stock and dead stock are brought to 'refit.' This establishment is the permanent headquarters of the show. Here the animals which need training are educated by the permanent trainer, who, if he is really clever at his work, can often pass his pupils on to other hands for actual exhibition in the show. One of these 'repositories' in North London is well worth a visit. Round the central hall runs a wide gallery, full of scenery, fittings, and appliances for shows past and future. With these are various deceased animals of note, stuffed, embalmed, or bottled in spirits of wine, according to size. This seems customary in foreign menageries. At the wedding of Pezon—the famous French menagerie owner and lion tamer — all the stuffed animals were brought in to decorate the breakfast salon. In Sanger's repository one or two skeletons of particular favourites are mounted for exhibition, *more* 'Jumbo's' bones. Below are the reserve of triumphal cars. Others are 'in dock,' being repainted and regilded. The artists who paint the cars are usually educated in the service of menageries, and by the united force of talent and the traditions of the profession have long been famous for their power of painting on the panels the most dreadful roaring, bounding, all-devouring lions which ever caught negroes under a palm-tree. Below on the ground-floor are the stalls and stables for the animals in hospital, on sick-leave, or simply needing rest and quiet. These quarters are kept in half-darkness, as the dim light suits animal invalids. The elephants are picketed by the leg. Other animals—zebras, llamas, goats, and camels —are kept in loose-boxes or pens made of high hurdles. Every morning all the animals on furlough are taken out for long walks, each being led by a lad or a keeper. It was when out for one of these constitutionals from the hospital that Sanger's big elephant ran away through Islington some years ago, and met with such remarkable adventures. The old-fashioned 'wild-beast shows' like Wombwell's, Maunder's, and others which delighted the country towns and villages thirty years ago by simply exhibiting animals in caravans, with a few elephants and camels to carry visitors, are now usually merged in circuses, in which the performances of trained animals have the first place. This demands a great number of horses and ponies. These have very hard work in the arena, especially those which are trained to jump over flights of hurdles. The regularity with which menagerie horses will 'come to the scratch,' sometimes twice daily, for a long series of gallops, broad jumps, and high jumps would surprise many owners of hunters whose mounts often knock up after very mild and occasional spells of work. Jumping four to six hurdles in and out, with two held one above the other to finish with, was a feat performed by one circus horse up to the age of sixteen. A week or two in the repository every six months was all the rest he required even at the end of his career. The number of animals travelling in a single troop without accident or sickness is surprising.

During a recent summer one hundred and sixty-three horses, with six elephants, several camels, ostriches, and emus, in Sanger's menagerie, travelled almost daily through the South-Midland and Southern counties, often spending the night, and giving an exhibition at by no means large provincial towns with considerable financial success. In one week they travelled by road —menageries do not patronize railways—from Newbury, along the Kennett Valley, to Reading; thence up the Thames Valley to Windsor, Staines, Kingston, and Epsom. At each place they gave two performances, in the morning and evening, besides making the journey. All the scenery, vans, and material of a huge tent, large enough to hold ten thousand people, were packed and transported, the draught-power being furnished by the animals attached to the show. For six weeks this show was certified to have earned an average of one thousand pounds a week, during which time it visited thirty-four different towns! If variety and change of scene are good for the animals' constitutions, they must have been in rude health at the end of this period. Most of the marching is done in the early morning. The elephants, camels, and other beasts of draught are taken, if possible, to a stream to drink; and nothing could well be more strangely in contrast to its surroundings than the group of camels and elephants drinking from a wayside stream, the former browsing on the hawthorn branches full of May blossom. With the rise of the circus element in menageries has come an additional demand for the 'taming' and training of wild and domestic animals. The trainer is not always the performer. There is no better proof of his success than when someone else can enter the cage and take his place, as when Madame Baptistine Pezon, when her husband fell ill, put on the costume he used in performances, and put the lions through their tricks. The demeanour of the animals themselves, when lions, tigers, or leopards perform, is often evidence of the method, whether cruel or kind, employed first in taming and later in teaching them. A correspondent of the *Globe*, recounting the history of the famous *dompteur*, states that lions are often tamed, like hawks, by deprivation of sleep, accompanied by plentiful feeding. It is very doubtful whether English trainers are cruel to animals. Mr.

Sanger makes the following ingenuous defence of his profession. 'I have trained everything in the business,' he writes, 'from the child to the elephant, and I would like to deny the slanderous things that have been written by inexperienced people, and to correct the idea of the ignorant, that everything belonging to circus life must be carried on by the arm of terror and cruelty. There may be isolated cases; but the people of my profession, I am proud to say, have the feelings of fathers and mothers. With regard to the training of children, the care and interest bestowed in the teaching of arduous tricks are really an education and the perfection of humanity; and with regard to the training of horses, a bit of sugar or a carrot is far more efficacious and more often used than the whip.' But horses are not wild beasts; and Pezon admitted that he never dared to take his eyes off those of his lions until he contrived to have some highly-charged electric wires between them and him. White bears are almost too dangerous to train at all. Some appeared in Hagenbeck's last sale catalogue; but even Pezon was nearly killed by one, and retired from training after the accident. His colleagues in the business claimed that *sangfroid* and courage were the main qualities in the success of the *dompteur*, and that the animals felt first surprise, then astonishment, and lastly fear of the man who did not fear them. But the highest class of 'lion-tamers' have qualities other than mere courage, part being, no doubt, an almost magnetic intuition of the working of the creature's mind, and the power of conveying impressions to the animal and engendering confidence. The old Irishman known as 'The Whisperer' was the classic instance of this kind of real tamer of savage animals. Pezon himself possessed it in a high degree, for he began his reputation as a pacifier of vicious horses and savage bulls in the village of Lozère.

XV.—ANIMALS IN FAMINE

The rains that announce the close of an Indian famine bring relief to animals before they lighten human sufferings. The green-stuff springs up and gives food for the cattle long before the grain can ripen and provide a meal for the peasant. But the animals have time to recover their strength and be ready to do their work in preparing the ground for the next crop, and the actual loss of life among the beasts of the field is arrested. This is said to have been less in the last famine than in many which have affected much smaller areas. The total failure of the grain crops was due to absence of rain at a definite point of time when it was necessary to its germination. But there was not such a protracted and general drought as to bring on the whole animal population a famine in the form which causes most suffering to it.

In their wild state most animals live under the incubus of two sources of terror—death by violence from their natural foe or foes, and death by famine.

The greater number are never far removed from the latter possibility; it is the inevitable sequence of disablement, weakness, or old age, and if not cut off by pestilence, violence or fatal accident, they have all to face this grim spectre in the closing scene. Yet in most cases dread of the latter is not present to their consciousness in the form of apprehension—only as shadowed out by actual reminder caused by scarcity of food at a particular time, or a total failure, which drives them to wander. But the fear of the 'natural enemy' is always vivid and oppressive, and alters the whole course of their everyday life. The deer on certain of the Highland mountains, exposed in any hard winter to almost inevitable famine, do not profit by experience of famine. Experience of danger from man makes them the most wary of animals; they sleep with waking senses, feed by night, are constantly under the influence of this besetting terror, and take every measure which experience suggests to guard against the enemy. Experience of famine leaves them no wiser than before. They do not abandon the spots in which they suffered in previous years until they actually feel the pinch of hunger, and they return to the same inhospitable ground when the scarcity has passed. Yet when confronted by the two terrors, hunger and man, they are simply insensible to the fear of the latter, usually so dominant. Starvation looms larger than any terror from living

Hard Times on Exmoor.

foes, and they invade the rickyards, and almost enter the dwellings, of their only hereditary enemy. Recent accounts of the behaviour of four thousand starving elk in the northern territory of the United States correspond exactly with those of the Highland deer in the hard winter of 1893. They approached the buildings for food, and could hardly be driven from the stacks of hay. Yet only one herbivorous animal out of all the multitude of species has ever thought of making a store of hay against a time of famine, and this is one of the most insignificant of all, the pika, or calling hare of the Russian steppes. There would be nothing very extraordinary in the fact if social animals, such as deer, cattle, or antelopes, did gather quantities of long herbage, like the tall grasses of Central Africa or of the Indian swamps, and accumulate it for the benefit of the herd, and combine to protect it from other herds, or if they reserved certain portions of the longer herbage for food in winter. The latter would perhaps demand a greater range of concepts than the former. But the brain-power of the improvident deer must be equal to that of the squirrel or field-mouse, which seldom forget to lay aside a 'famine fund.' In temperate climates, prolonged frost or snow is the only frequent cause of famine among either beasts or birds. This cause is not constant, season by season, but it occurs often enough in the lifetime of most individuals of the different species to impress their memory by suffering. In the plains of India, and even more regularly in the plains of Africa, the summer heats cause partial famine to all herbivorous animals, and this condition is recurring and constant. Brehm has described the cumulative suffering of the animal world of the 'African steppe,' mainly from famine, at the close of this regular period of summer drought. We cannot suppose that in this case the terror of starvation is wholly forgotten in the brief time of plenty. The neglect to form any store, or to reserve pastures in climates sufficiently temperate to spare them from being burnt up with summer heat, suggests the question whether these 'hand-to-mouth' herbivorous animals rely on any natural reserves of food not obvious to us. This is a natural device, exemplified by the Kaffir, who, when his mealies fail, lives on roots and grubs, or by the insect and vegetable-eating rook, which becomes carnivorous in a drought. To some extent both deer and cattle do rely on such reserves. When the grass is burnt up, trees are still luxuriant, and it is to the woods that the ruminant animals look as a reserve in famine. The fact was recognised during the siege of Paris, when all the trees of the boulevards and the parks were felled late in September that the tens of thousands of cattle might browse on the young shoots and leaves. It is this habit of hungry cattle which makes the space under all trees in parks of the same height—that to which cattle can lift their heads to bite the branches. When the wood or forest has been enclosed previously, the whole of this stock of food, reaching down to the ground, instead of to the 'cattle line,' is at their service. Sir Dietrich Brandis, lately chief of the Forest Department of the Indian Empire, makes special mention of the part played by this 'reserve' in the economy of animal famines in India. During the years of drought and famine in 1867 and 1868, the cattle (of all the inhabitants) were allowed to graze in the Rajah's preserves at Rupnagar. The branches of the trees were cut for fodder. The same was done in Kishangarh, and a large proportion of the cattle of these two places were preserved during those terrible years.

But there are regions, like the African steppe, where the summer famines among animals are more frequent than in India, and where there is little forest available as a reserve store of food. Certain animals 'trek' for great distances to escape from the famine area. Birds leave it entirely. But the greater number of the quadrupeds stay and take their chance, the stronger of hunger, the weak of famine and death.

If we examine the stores made by most of the vegetable-eating animals which do lay by a 'famine fund,' we find a rather curious similarity in the food commonly used by them. They nearly all live on vegetable substances in a concentrated form—natural food-lozenges, which are very easily stored away. There is a great difference, for example, between the bulk of nutriment eaten in the form of grass by a rabbit, and the same amount of sustenance in the 'special preparation' in the kernel of a nut, or the stone of a peach, or the bulb of a crocus, off which a squirrel makes a meal. Nearly all the storing animals eat 'concentrated food,' whether it be beans and grain, hoarded by the hamster, or nuts and hard fruits, by the squirrel, nuthatch, and possibly some of the jays. But there is one vegetable-eating animal whose food is neither concentrated nor easy to move. On the contrary, it is obtained with great labour in the first instance, and stored with no less toil after it is procured. The beaver lives during the winter on the bark of trees. As it is not safe, and often impossible, for the animal to leave the water when the ice has formed, it stores these branches under water, cutting them into lengths, dragging them below the surface, and fixing them down to the bottom with stones and mud. This is more difficult work than gathering hay.

Birds, in spite of their powers of locomotion, suffer greatly from famine. Many species which could leave the famine area seem either deficient in the instinct to move, or unwilling to do so. Rooks, for instance, which are now known to migrate across the Channel

A BEAVER IN THE WATER.

and the North Sea, will hang about the same parish in bad droughts and suffer acutely, though they might easily move to places where water, if not food, is abundant. The frost famines mainly affect the insect-eating birds; and as these live on animal food, which would not keep, they could not be expected to make a store. But there is no such difference of possible food between birds which do make stores and birds which do not. Why, for instance, should the nuthatch and the Mexican woodpecker lay by for hard times while the rook does not?

Domestic animals in this country are very properly guaranteed by recent legislation against being left to starve by their owners. It is not often that the owner of any domesticated animal is so careless of his own interests as to neglect to provide food when the creature is capable of work, or so inhuman if it is not. But instances do occur to the contrary. The law does recognise an implied right on the part of the animal to this exemption from the great curse of animal existence, if man has exacted from it a previous tribute in the form of work. But there is a borderland of animal domestication in which this implicit duty of man to beast is seriously neglected, partly because the work done by the animal is less obvious, though it is kept for the profit of man. There are great areas of new country in Argentina, the United States, and

Australia where the raising of stock, whether sheep, cattle, or horses, is carried on without much regard to the limits set by famine in years of frost or drought. The creatures are multiplied without regard to famine periods, and no reserve of food is kept to meet these. Natural laws are left to work in bad times, and this 'natural law' is death by famine. Consequently, at times we hear of multitudes of starving horses on the ranches of Oregon; and in Australia during a drought, or in Argentina after protracted drought or cold, sheep and cattle die by tens of thousands by the most lingering of deaths. There is something amiss here in the relations between man and beast which cannot be justified even on 'business' grounds.

XVI.—PLAGUE-STRUCK ANIMALS

EVIDENCE of the intensity and virulence of the late plague in Bombay is given by the curious accounts telegraphed to this country of the deaths of animals from the pestilence. At one period it was reported that the pigeons were dying of plague. Later the rats were said to have been plague-stricken, and to be dying in thousands in the native town, and there was strong evidence that they not only suffered from plague, but spread the infection.

If those who were fighting the plague had time to attend to anything but the work of saving human life, we may expect more curious information on this point ; for there is evidence that when the plague was at its very worst in Florence, causing the death of sixty thousand persons, the pestilence acquired some kind of cumulative energy by which it went on from man to animals, and at last involved the latter in common destruction with their masters. As it advanced, ' not only men but animals fell sick and shortly expired, if they had touched things belonging to the diseased or dead.' Boccaccio himself saw two hogs on the rags of a person who had died of plague, after staggering about for a short time, fall down dead as if they had taken poison. In the 'Lives of the Roman Pontiffs' it is stated that in other places multitudes of cats, dogs, fowls and other animals fell victims to the contagion. There is little doubt that this concurrence of human and animal death took place in other countries than Italy, though the chroniclers, appalled by the loss of human life, only allude to 'murrain' among the cattle as a concomitant of the plague. 'At the commencement of the Black Death there was in England,' says Hecker,* 'an abundance of all the necessaries of life; but the plague, which seemed then to be the sole disease, was soon accompanied by a fatal murrain among the cattle. Wandering about without herdsmen, they fell by thousands.' It is not known whether this murrain was due to plague itself or to some special animal epidemic. But it did not break out until after the plague was rife, and added enormously to the loss of life, because it was impossible to remove the corn from the fields, this causing everywhere a great rise in the price of food, although the harvest had been plentiful. Whether it affected wild beasts as well as domesticated animals does not appear; but in only

* 'Epidemics of the Middle Ages.'

one instance do we hear of an increase in their numbers, such as might naturally be expected to follow the destruction of human life. After a plague epidemic in France in 1503, the house-dogs became wild, and later, communal hunts were organized to rid the country of these new beasts of prey, and of the wolves, which appeared in great packs.

It is not known whether the animals of Florence, like those of Bombay, were really suffering from plague. But there is good reason to believe that their deaths were connected by something more than coincidence of time with the plague epidemic. What the old physicians called 'general morbific conditions'—that change of atmosphere and temperature which seems to summon pestilence full-grown from the very ground in certain parts of the East—apparently prepared animal constitutions to receive the human disease. A month before the cholera became rife in Hamburg, sixty per cent. of Carl Hagenbeck's animals suffered from choleraic symptoms; and he diagnosed the disease, checked it by boiling the water, and notified the authorities of what had happened. The curious exactness with which Homer noted that in the plague before Troy, mules and dogs were attacked before the soldiers, has often been quoted as internal evidence of the truth of the 'Iliad.' Influenza, which was very fatal among animals, sometimes attacked them before it was felt by men, as in New York, where it first appeared among the horses. In London, horses, cats, dogs, pigeons, parrots and penguins died of influenza. In the year 1800, when yellow fever reached Cadiz and Seville, dogs took the disease more freely than other animals; but cats, horses, poultry and cage-birds also died. The symptoms in the case of the dogs and cats resembled those in man. The animals were not attacked until the deaths among men numbered two hundred a day. In 1830, when the cattle, fowls and geese of South Russia died of cholera, the appearance of the disease was also subsequent to its development among human beings.

Animal epidemics taking place simultaneously with human pestilence are immensely aggravated by the impossibility of separating infected and non-infected cattle. The herdsmen die, and the flocks and herds run wild. But this does not account for the deadly character of animal epidemics in general, or for the little resistance offered by animal constitutions to such diseases. Human beings are usually prepared by long unwholesome living. Compare the account of the Bombay native house—dark, with the floor soaked with dirt, and the *free* water left always dripping from the tap by the inmates—and Erasmus's description of the floor of an English cottage, 'made of nothing but loam, and strewed with rushes, which being constantly put on fresh, without a removal of the old, remain lying there, in some cases twenty years, with fish-bones, broken victuals, and other filth,' and impregnated with liquid nastiness. But though chicken-cholera and other epidemics of poultry are mainly due to unwholesome surroundings, the life of most domestic animals, especially cattle, and of all wild animals, such as antelopes and the wild bovines, is exceptionally healthy. Except in famine years, there is no predisposing cause to make them succumb to pestilence as they do. Even when untended, so that the separation of infected animals is impossible, or when wild, such cattle or deer separate themselves by instinct from the herd and remain alone. Isolation is voluntary. What should prove another great factor in protecting animal life in epidemics is the absence of those nervous terrors which always predispose human beings to infection, and often cause death itself by the mere horror of anticipation. Fear, contrition, religious mania, despondency, grief, despair, drink and delirium, and the break-up of the normal social order, swelled the list of human deaths in the epidemics of the Middle Ages, and some of these factors aggravate the incidence of every great plague among mankind. It is not so with animals. Their naturally healthy frames are impaired by no nervous terrors or morbid mental affections in the presence of disease. Though some of the more intelligent are distressed at the deaths of their masters, they exhibit great indifference to wholesale mortality among their own species. Yet with every chance in their favour they succumb to pestilence in a manner quite unaccountable. The statistics of the rinderpest epidemic in South Africa will probably never be forthcoming. Its general results, so far as Matabeleland is concerned, are well known. They indicate the total destruction, so far as transport and food are concerned, of the domestic cattle of the country. With them, over large areas, the antelopes and other ruminants have perished. The reason of this great mortality has never been explained, though the main source of infection—at least, in countries where cattle or game run wild, is obvious. It is at the drinking-places that all animals, infected or sound, necessarily meet, however much the former may desire to wander away in solitude. This was proved in part during the cattle-plague in this country, where certain farms in which the herds were watered from protected wells, and never allowed to drink from the streams, continued free from the disease.

As a set-off to the rapid mortality of animals in plagues, the rate of their subsequent recovery in numbers must be taken into account. The subject now most anxiously debated in South Africa is the time which must elapse before the herds of cattle are replenished. The time will probably be less than the most sanguine could anticipate. Destructive as they are at the time, plagues leave no such far-reaching results among animals as among men. It is in the period subsequent to pestilence that the simplicity of their lives gains by contrast. They have no social life to be disorganized, no nexus of trade to be broken, no famine to fear from untilled fields, no general weakening of the race from inherited weakness and nervous disorders transmitted for generations from parents who never fully recovered the 'plague terror.' The mental shock transmitted by the Black Death produced nervous disorders for two centuries—the dancing mania from Norway to Abyssinia, convulsions, hysteria, delusions of all sorts, aggravated by famine and poverty, the direct results of the plague. For animals, on the contrary, there are no nervous *sequelæ* to an epidemic. The race is improved rather than impaired, for the aged, the weak, and the unfit are dead, and only the strong parents survive. The increase in fecundity—an increase noted even among the surviving European population after the Black Death—is very great, and in place of being checked by famine due to untilled fields, is fostered by the surplus of natural food for a reduced number of mouths.

XVII.—THE ANIMAL 'CHAPTER OF ACCIDENTS'

THE midnight passages of great flocks of birds over large cities which from time to time have attracted the attention of naturalists usually leave no trace of the visits of the fowl, which vanish as soon as the dawn appears. Though the calls of the birds and the sound of their wings may indicate that vast numbers and various species, such as herons, gulls, plovers, crows, terns, ducks, geese, and small birds, have hovered for hours over cities, as has been noted both at Norwich and Leicester on a ' migration night,' with the dawn of day the spell is broken, and the flocks resume their journey without leaving a single bird behind. The Manchester papers record a curious mishap which befell some large bird recently, probably while making one of these midnight flights. The Manchester Town Hall is surmounted by a spiked ball ; and on one of the spikes of this finial, at a height of nearly three hundred feet, a bird, said by some to be an eagle, and identified by others as a heron, was seen to be firmly impaled. An enterprising owner of a big telescope fixed it up to oblige those of his customers who wished to discover what species of fowl met with this curious death, one which is, we believe, unparalleled in the animal 'chapter of accidents.'

If the 'bills of mortality' in the animal world could be made out with precision, and the causes ascertained, accidents would, we think, account for a much smaller number of deaths than might be expected, or, indeed, desired, if the accidents were immediately fatal; for such sudden death would save them from that grim spectre of lingering starvation which lurks in the background of the life of most of the higher animals. But accidental death, or death hastened by injuries due to accidents, is not very common among wild animals, while domesticated species, though much more liable to injure themselves, have the enormous privilege of 'first aid to the wounded' accorded them by man.

Birds are naturally the least liable to accidents of any living creatures.* This immunity they owe almost entirely to the fact that the air in which most of their movements take place is absolutely free from obstacles to flight at a height of four hundred feet above the

* But after the recent hurricane in the West Indies it was found that every bird and almost every insect was dead. The islands were absolutely silent, as the hum of insect and bird life had ceased entirely.

ground. The only objects against which collision is possible are other birds; and this possibility is reduced to a minimum because they are not limited to any one plane, or even to one deep 'layer,' of the air for flight. Compared with the case of the terrestrial animals, all moving on the single level of the land surface, just as ships move on the one plane of the sea surface, the birds ought not to be liable to collision at all; and it is their theoretical freedom from this danger which makes the high rate of bird-speed possible, a speed denied to other animals, if for no other reason, because, moving as they do on a single plane, they would be as liable to disabling collision as autocars running at express speed on Southsea Common. The sole risk of collision is when flocks are travelling together. As the direction is then usually the same, and the birds take most careful precautions to avoid danger by maintaining regular distance, an even speed, and often a kind of military order, such mishaps are rare. They chiefly occur when birds which 'get up steam' at once are rising from the ground. Partridges and grouse are most commonly liable to this accident, and instances are recorded every season; but even small birds are occasionally 'in collision,' the most unusual instance recently noted being that of a pair of greenfinches, one of which flew against the other and broke a wing. The windows of lighthouses and telegraph-wires, though causing very numerous accidents to birds, should properly be regarded as unintended traps. They are as much 'fixed engines' for bird-killing as nets or snares, for the creatures are dazzled by the former, and at night are quite unable to see the latter. The only other accident common to birds is confined to some species of water-fowl, especially moorhens and dabchicks. These are commonly killed by ice, both by diving under it when newly formed and rising to the surface where clear ice covers it, or by being frozen in by their feet. This, which sounds improbable, is a very common mishap, especially to moorhens, whose large feet are with difficulty withdrawn when pinched by the ice.

Among wild quadrupeds, only the ruminants with large horns and long limbs seem commonly liable to accidents. Cases of stags dying with interlocked antlers are recorded from time to time, and Buckland gives an account of a curious accident which befell a big stag in Windsor Forest. The poor beast had been standing on its hind-legs to nibble leaves from a thorn-tree, and caught its hoof in a fork in the trunk. This threw it on its back and broke the bone. Though red-deer are in this country mainly found wild on mountainous ground, we much doubt if they are really a mountain species, or specially clever on rocky ground. Mr. J. G. Millais mentions one pass where the bones of deer that have missed their footing and fallen down the crags may frequently be seen. Broken limbs are very common, even among park stags, generally due to fights in the rutting time. This must usually lead to the death of deer in all districts where large carnivora are found; but the astonishing way in which broken bones, or even worse injuries received by wild animals, cure themselves if the creature is let alone, shows that the most serious accidents need not lead to death, even if left to nature. The most striking of recent instances is the case of a doe antelope at Leonardslee, which smashed its hind-leg high up, and so badly that the bone protruded. It would have been shot, but it was observed to be feeding as if not in pain. It survived the winter, and was seen to *swing the injured leg forward to scratch its ear* before the bone set. The fracture reduced itself, and the cut skin grew over the place, leaving a scar. Later, though lame, it was perfectly well, and reared a young one. A tiger, recently killed in the hot weather, had a bullet-wound a week old which had smashed its shoulder. This wound, though a very bad one, was perfectly healthy, and there was evidence that since it was inflicted the tiger had eaten no flesh, but only drunk water. In the Waterloo Cup coursing in 1886, Miss Glendyne and the 'runner-up' for the cup were slipped at a hare which went wild and strong. When killed after a good course by the two crack greyhounds, it was found to have only three feet. This may be compared with the accounts of a collie-dog, recently quoted in the papers, which had one fore-foot and one hind-foot cut off by a reaping-machine, but which still manages to help with the flock. Dogs, which ought to be little liable to accidents, are very frequent sufferers, largely from their association with man and intense desire to participate in all his doings. One of their commonest mishaps arises from their love of riding in carts. They become quite clever at scrambling or jumping in, but are not 'built' for jumping down on to a hard road. If the cart moves as they make their spring the danger is increased, and fore-legs broken, usually just below the shoulder, are very commonly seen. Dogs also have dangerous falls when on the ground, accidents usually ascribed only to bipeds and horses. A greyhound going at full speed will trip, fly head over heels, and break a leg, or even its neck. Master Magrath in 1870 went through the rotten ice of the river Alt, from which Altcar takes its name, while following the hare, and nearly died from the effects. But the strangest mishap which the writer has ever seen fall to the lot of a dog was the case of a setter which 'tripped' over a sitting hare. The dog, a large, heavy animal, was ranging at high speed in a field of thinly-planted mangold. As it passed between the rows its hind-feet struck something, and it nearly turned a somersault.

The object was a squatting hare, which, as the dog flew over in one direction, quietly scuttled off in the other. It is difficult to find a reason for the liability even of 'heather sheep,' as well as of the more domestic varieties, to death by falls over cliffs, and even by being thrown and unable to rise. They seem to have lost more of their inherited capacity for mountaineering than could be expected from the slight structural changes caused in the wild sheep by domestication. We do not recollect a single recorded instance of accident from falls in the case of the wild varieties of sheep, though the domestic breeds seem to have been liable to these and other accidents from the days of the 'ram caught by the horns' on the mountain in the land of Moriah.

XVIII.—THIRSTY ANIMALS

AMONG the questions asked in relation to the difficulties of the latest Indian Frontier War was the reason why the difficulty of obtaining water blocked our advance, but did not hamper the hillmen. The answer is that our troops had in one camp upwards of twenty-five thousand baggage animals. There were oxen, mules, donkeys, and camels. The former are always thirsty creatures, and even the camels are credited with vastly larger powers of sustaining thirst than they possess. Major A. G. Leonard, after seventeen years' experience as a transport officer, is convinced that camels should, if possible, be watered every day, that they cannot be trained to do without water, and that, though they can retain one and a half gallons of water in the cells of the stomach, four or five days' abstinence is as much as they can stand, in heat and with dry food, without permanent injury.

It is very doubtful whether the majority of the various 'desert animals' willingly go without water,

or, in fact, do so at all to any great extent. They
drink sparingly, and can probably, by habit and practice,
go for longer periods without drinking than species
living in well-watered districts. But the absence of
any special provision for the internal storing of water,
except in the camels and some tortoises, seems to
indicate that this power of temporary abstinence is
only an acquired capacity. Nor is it often possible to
be certain that stores of water do not exist in 'deserts'—
stores perfectly well known to the animals, though not
to travellers. This is especially the case in rocky
deserts such as the Bayuda Desert, and that between
Suakin and Berber. Some of the correspondents of the
London daily papers who recently made the journey
from the advanced posts on the Nile to Suakin noted
as remarkable that, though they were in a desert, and
making forced marches from want of water, which,
when found, was as black as ink and almost undrink-
able, hares and gazelles swarmed. This is an almost
certain sign that this desert is not waterless. Count
Gleichen, when recrossing the Bayuda Desert from
Metemmeh, found real cisterns of water in one place
away from the ordinary track. A typical desert-bird,
which, like the gazelles, jerboas, and sand-lizards, has
even taken its colour from its environment, is the sand-
grouse. Yet Mr. Bryden states that the daily flight
of the sand-grouse, a species of exceedingly swift and

swallow-like flight, to the water is one of the sights of the veldt in the dry season. 'Their machine-like punctuality, and the wonderful displays afforded by their enormous flights at the desert-pools,' form the subject of one of Mr. Bryden's chapters in his recent work on South Africa. 'The watering process is gone through with perfect order and without over-crowding. From eight o'clock to close on ten this wonderful flight continued; as birds drank and departed, others were constantly arriving to take their places. I should judge that the average time spent by each bird at and around the water was half an hour.' A curious instance or animal knowledge of the presence of water in unsuspected places had a practical result in Holland. The question of a supply of good water for the Hague was under discussion at the time when the North Sea Canal was being constructed. One of those present remarked that there was water in the sand-hills; that the hares, rabbits, and partridges which swarm in the sand-hills did *not* come to the wet 'polders' to drink, but knew of some supply in the 'dunes' themselves, and that he could name one or two places where he had seen water. This idea was laughed at; but one of the local engineers present took the hint. The dunes were carefully explored, and the result was the cutting of a long reservoir in the centre of the sand-hills, which fills with water naturally, and supplies the town.

It is believed that rabbits can exist *in this climate* without a permanent water-supply. Where they are kept in enclosed warrens without water this must be accepted as a fact. The writer has only seen one such warren, and in this there are always plenty of drinking-troughs for the young pheasants in summer, though in winter the rabbits can only find rain-water and dew. Those in this warren are very poor and small. Tame rabbits are commonly kept without water, but they may be seen licking the bars of their hutch after a shower, and drink eagerly when they have the chance. Most other rodents, including rats, are thirsty creatures. The only animals living in very dry places which seem able to do entirely without drink are snakes and reptiles. In the *cold* desert of shifting sand in Kashgar there are no reptiles, and not even a fly. But the Afghan Boundary Commission found swarms of lizards and a new and venomous species of adder in astonishing numbers in the awful desert of *hot* shifting sand at the corner where Persia, Baluchistan, and Afghanistan meet. We must note one exception, the giraffe, which, Mr. Bryden believes, exists for three-quarters of the year in the North Kalahari without water. But this cannot be proved until the desert has been explored, and the total absence of water confirmed. There is known to be water beneath the surface ; and if the giraffe does live waterless, he must imbibe his liquid nutriment at second-hand in the juices of the leaves of the trees which have their roots in the moisture. Seals, apparently, do not drink, neither do cormorants and penguins; but there can be little more evaporation from their bodies than from those of fish, and their food is wet and moist. A more difficult question is that of the water-supply of Arctic animals in winter— possibly they eat snow. There is abundant evidence that, though many animals can exist without water for long periods, this abstinence is not voluntary, and when unduly protracted causes suffering and loss of health. The whole cat tribe are proverbially 'tough,' and can not only recover from frightful bodily injuries, but endure hunger and thirst longer than most animals. Instances of cats lost or stuck fast in hollow walls, where, in addition to deprivation of food, they have been cut off from water for periods of a fortnight or more, are not uncommon, yet the cats have soon recovered; but it would be absolutely wrong to conclude that the animal did not suffer during its imprisonment, and the height of cruelty to compel it to face such deprivation. The normal habits of animals are a certain guide to their physical requirements, and the fondness of cats for water otherwise than for outside application ought to be matter of common knowledge. From the tiger, who regularly goes off for a 'long drink' after a kill, and commonly bathes in hot weather, to the household pussy, they all drink water regularly, the latter two or three times a day. The writer has often watched from the high-level railways the London cats belonging to the small tenements taking their mid-day drink of water in hot weather. They spring from the dividing walls on to the small water-cisterns, alighting neatly on the space between the cover of the cistern and the wall, and, leaning over, lap the water. Many people imagine that cats prefer milk to quench their thirst, and never provide them with water-pans. This is a mistake ; the cats, like the tigers and jaguars, prefer water, and the numerous cases of cats upsetting and breaking flower-vases on tables are usually due, not to mischief, but to the cat's efforts to drink the water in which the flowers are set. It is noticed that Persian cats are more eager for water than others. Experience shows that horses must not be allowed to drink freely before or immediately after hard riding or driving ; but this, too, is in keeping with their natural, or perhaps we should say their acquired, habits when originally wild. If, as is probably the case, the wild horses lived in the Central Asian steppes, like the kiang, or Central Asian wild ass, water can never have been plentiful ; and, like the African antelopes and zebras, the originals of the species probably drank only once in the twenty-four hours, going to considerable distances to obtain water. Another probable survival is the horse's dislike to drinking very cold water. It is commonly said that horses like pond-water and 'dirty' water. What they really like is water with the chill off; cold spring-water disagrees with them. Moreover, they are mighty particular as to the taste of their drinking-water. Some years ago one of several horses refused to drink his water, and was at once pronounced to be 'ill.' This caused inquiry, and it transpired that one of the children had *washed a guinea-pig* in this horse's bucket. The horse would not drink the guinea-pig's bath-water. In the same way cows, though less select in their choice of drinking-water than is desirable for those who consume their milk, dislike touching water from tubs from which a dog has drunk, and will refuse it altogether if a dog has bathed in it. The Turks always allow their horses to drink as much as they please, and when they please, and the Osmanli were always accustomed to make long journeys on horseback. But the more intelligent Arabs, than whom no race except the English has paid more attention to the subject, give their horses little water—a practice they follow themselves. A paste of flour, dates, a little water and camel's milk, is among many tribes the staple food for the desert horse. But we may say of him and his master, 'The wilderness and the barren land are his dwelling; he scorneth the multitude of the city.' He is a born 'abstainer,' even from excess in water-drinking.

XIX.—THE EFFECT OF HEAT ON ANIMALS

THOUGH 'iced beds' cooled by a warming-pan filled with ice are now recommended as a means to secure sleep by night in hot weather, the effect of a rise in temperature on the comfort of the animal world is not yet discussed in the newspapers. Yet it is worthy of remark that the conditions under which wild and domesticated animals face sudden waves of heat are very different. Most beasts of burden and draught animals have to do as much work when the temperature is above eighty degrees in the shade as in ordinary weather, and in some cases even more, for heat makes their masters less willing to walk themselves. In New York sunstroke is very common among the omnibus and tram horses. In Bombay an ingenious sun-helmet has been invented to protect the back of the head and first vertebra of the neck in horses compelled to work when the sun is hot. The tram-horses, generally either 'Walers' or from Central Asia, suffer both from headache and sunstroke, and now wear a hat, through which the ears project. It is fastened under the horse's chin by strings, and gives him a curiously civilized and un-Oriental air. In London our omnibus companies 'stand drinks' to their animals in exceptionally hot weather. The favourite beverage is oatmeal and water. The horses know the stages at which this will be supplied, and show the greatest eagerness to get it.

English harness, though excellent for cool weather, is very trying to horses in the great heat. The multiplicity of straps and the hot collar form a network of wet, hot lines across the animal's back and flanks. Soldiers sweating under the pressure of cross-belts and side-belts on a summer march soon realize the feelings of the over-harnessed horses, and take the view that the light American harness, worked with a breast-plate in place of a collar, is probably far more comfortable for the animal. The violent perspiration of some horses, though it looks uncomfortable, is in all likelihood a relief to them. There is nothing worse for a horse than to be 'hide-bound,' and the only discomforts which the opposite symptoms entail are the danger of sores being caused by harness rubbing on the wet skin, and the risk of chills, to which horses are equally subject with human beings in hot weather. One driver of the writer's acquaintance always maintained that one of his horses could sweat at pleasure, and did so whenever he wanted to shirk work. 'He's artful, he's artful,' was the invariable reply, if the condition of the animal's coat were pointed out as a reason for moderating the pace. Nervous exhaustion from heat is probably more common among horses than is supposed. They suffer not only from the depression of tone caused by the temperature, but from the worry and excitement induced by flies and insects, which madden the working horse, with no time or means to rid himself of them effectually. The network jackets and flaps granted even to smart carriage-horses in hot weather are a real benefit to them, and if cows could be provided with similar but more extensive protection, it is certain that the yield of milk would be increased by the respite from constant nervous worry. That it is the flies which accompany heat, rather than the heat itself, from which animals suffer when wild, or domesticated animals when at rest, seems proved by their habits in the New Forest. There the wild ponies and cattle all leave the woods in the mid-day heat and congregate in what are known as 'shades.' But these 'shades' are shadowless, being generally some quite open and elevated spot with no trees near and in the full glare of the sun. There, however, the tree-haunting flies and gnats are fewer, and if there is a breeze it can usually be felt. They prefer to face the heat to enduring the heat-insects, and more especially the crawling New-

Forest fly. In ordinary meadow-land cattle collect under trees towards mid-day, and in the afternoon, if it be possible, gather in the ponds, where they stand so deep that the lower and most sensitive parts of their bodies are completely covered by water. They thus gain coolness and protection from insects at the same time ; but there are not many field-ponds which are so large or accessible from the bank that cattle can enjoy themselves in this way, which, as Gilbert White remarked, was equally good both for the beasts and for the fish which gather round to catch the flies. During the great drought two summers ago horses became almost aquatic animals where this was possible. They waded shoulder-deep in the Thames, eating water-plants and seeking coolness, and, emboldened by these excursions, even swam the river and invaded the fields beyond. In the same year a small, deep pond in a meadow beyond Hanwell, visible from the Great Western Railway line, was used as a bath by four horses for the greater part of each day. They stood in it with the water almost level with their backs, and presented the appearance of huge river animals of the tapir kind floating in the pool. It seems clear from this that they derive the same refreshment from the application of cold water to the skin which other perspiring animals do. Humane cab-drivers recognise this fact by driving their horses as nearly as possible into the shower from the rear of a watering-cart, and there is little doubt that an occasional sluicing from a hose-pipe would probably do much for the health of the draught-horse in the dog-days. Deer both bathe and seek a draught in such weather. On one very hot day lately a red-deer hind took possession of an islet in Penn Pond in Richmond Park, swimming there and back, and spending the greater part of the morning in Robinson Crusoe fashion on the damp islet. Sheep do not suffer from the highest temperature of the English climate if shorn and left quiet with plenty of water. But any driving or travelling causes them the utmost distress at such times, and a careful shepherd prefers to make the common and daily change of pasture early in the morning or late in the evening. Dogs do not often die of sunstroke, but if made to work in great heat have violent fits and foaming at the mouth. Spaniels, if used for rabbiting in September, are very liable to these fits, and are cured by pouring cold water on the head and back of the neck. 'Mad dog!' is the silly cry usually raised on these occasions, though there is not the least cause for alarm, as the flow of saliva is quite harmless. When lying about the house at their ease individual dogs seem to take different views of the effects of hot weather. Most seek some cool material to lie on—tiles or grass for choice, rather than rugs or mats. They also lie on their sides with their legs

Cool Quarters. Highland Cattle.

extended, to admit the air to as much of the skin as possible, instead of lying curled up to exclude air, as in winter. Some seek a draughty passage, or lie at an open window, and nearly all revel in a bathe. Curiously enough, however much a dog enjoys a swim in hot weather, it scarcely ever goes off of its own accord away from the house to take one. The writer once owned a setter which would do this. But as a rule, though they know where the water is, and will in dry localities run away half a mile when out for a walk in order to take a dip, they do not leave the house by themselves to have a bathe. Cats *never* bathe,* though tigers do so regularly in the Indian heats, and will sit for a long time up to their necks in water. But the cat seems to rejoice in any degree of heat, and to be willing to sit in a cucumber-frame or a greenhouse, or on a lead roof, on the hottest days of the year. On the other hand, they become very thirsty in such weather, and need water. Mr. Hagenbeck, the owner of the Thier Park at Hamburg, has found that his Polar bears actually enjoy the hottest sun of midsummer, and lie out exposed to its rays when other animals are distressed by the heat. On the hottest day which he remembers to have felt in Hamburg he went round the gardens at mid-day to see if the animals needed any

* A correspondent writes to say that he had a cat which did this; but I leave the words as above.

special treatment. Cases of human sunstroke had been dropping in at the hospitals all the morning, and he was not surprised to find both a tiger and a leopard in a fit, and almost insensible. But the polar bear had left its inner cage, and stretched itself flat on the hot stones, where it could enjoy to the full the excessive heat of the North German midsummer.

All birds seem to enjoy the heat, provided that they can obtain water, which in this country is never wanting except on the chalk downs when the ponds dry up. There the rooks wait till dusk round the troughs from which the sheep are watered, evidently suffering acutely from thirst. But pigeons will seek out the hottest slopes and angles of the roofs; and common roadside birds, such as the yellow-hammers and pipits, sit out in the sun all day. Most of the insect-eating birds, except the fly-catchers, retire to the trees and bushes, and both chickens and partridges purposely seek shade. The former, if no other cover is available, will lie in the shadow of a wall, creeping close up to it as the line of shade narrows towards mid-day. Partridges either lie under the hedges or move into the turnip-fields when, as in hot September weather, the leaves are broad enough to cover them. But our wild birds never suffer from heat like those of Australia, where the parrots and lories have been seen to drop down dead when forced to fly across the open ground in a summer drought.

XX.—ANIMALS IN THE DARK

When a thick fog descends on London, it often stops like a blanket just above the summit of the ordinary buildings, though the tops of the towers and great hotels are covered with darkness. All the pigeons and sea-gulls, which are sitting on the towers and pediments, or soaring over the river, hasten to descend into the light; and while the former settle on the lower ledges and cornices, the latter skim over the Thames below the fog-belt, where they can see the world around them.

Thick fog bewilders all animals; and in real darkness —that is, in total absence of light—they are no more able to see than man. In the 'Mammoth Caves' they lost their eyes, as they do in the deep seas; and even in the catacombs below Paris there are signs that some such change would in time take place. But the power of sight in what we term 'the dark' is the rule, and not the exception, among the great majority of animals. The list of those which are either unable to find their way, or feed, or move freely by night, is a short one ; and its chief interest lies in the difficulty of accounting for their dependence upon sunlight, while to other and nearly allied creatures night is as clear as day.

Among wild birds, other than those which feed by night, all the hawks, pheasants, finches and buntings are almost helpless in the dark, sleep heavily, and are easily caught. Why, then, are the wood-pigeon, the rook, and most of the small warblers perfectly alert when once awakened at night, and able to fly through woods and cover as easily as by day? Pheasants may almost be picked off a tree by night, and are so helpless that if they are driven down they often cannot see to fly up again; sparrows and finches cannot see a bat-fowling net, and trained hawks are quite helpless, and have even been killed in the dark by rats, which the hawks would eat themselves by day. Tame pigeons are also helpless in the dark, or are so sleepy that they do not know what they are doing. On the other hand, wood-pigeons disturbed at night will dart off through boughs and branches without hesitation or accident. Common fowls are perfectly helpless at night, while guinea-fowls are as quick-sighted as a plover.

Among wild quadrupeds it is difficult to name one which cannot see in the dark. From the elephant to the hare they seem equally alert by night; and even the prairie-dogs, in spite of their anxiety to be in bed by dark, are most alert if they are turned out of bed into a dark room.

There is evidence that, in spite of their ability to find their way and to feed by night, animals are not exempt from some forms of nervousness induced by darkness. How far this affects the individual animal it is difficult to tell; but its effect is seen in the panics which seize on animals at night, panics which seldom, if ever, occur during the daytime. Whether these night-panics occur among the wild animals that live in companies and herds we have no sufficient means of ascertaining; but among domesticated creatures these terrors of the night are not uncommon, and in some cases lead to serious mischief. The most remarkable instance which has occurred in late years in this country was some sudden terror which affected the sheep on the hills reaching from the downs west of Reading to the Chiltern Hills. Reports came in from a very large number of parishes that the flocks had that night broken loose from their folds and scattered over the fields. The cause for so widespread a panic was never ascertained, but it is well known that sheep are liable to these frights by night. The commonest cause is the appearance near the fold of strange dogs, or even of an unknown man. Horses are also very liable to be 'stampeded' in the dark. Such mishaps are not common in this country, as when horses are in any numbers together they are usually kept in stables; but near Colchester some years ago the horses of several troops of cavalry, picketed for the night, took fright, pulled up their pickets, and suffered most severely in their gallop with the picket ropes and pins still attached. It is very doubtful whether the absence of daylight contributed much to the injuries received by the horses. The celebrated midnight steeplechase of the officers of a cavalry regiment stationed at Ipswich, in 1839, shows that horses can see by night when ridden at full speed. This freak, in the performance of which, though there was moonlight at intervals, the riders wore white night-gowns and night-caps that they might be able to see each other, led to no serious disasters either to horses or riders. As the latter could have done little to guide their mounts, or to pull them together for jumps the size of which they could not judge, we must assume that the horses could see as well as was necessary to clear a hedge and ditch. They also jumped a turnpike-gate on the main road, though this was perhaps more easily distinguished than the fences. On the pampas at night wild horses often try to stampede trained animals tethered round camps, and the Indians of the plains constantly avail themselves of the nervousness of horses at night to effect the same object. They either drive a mob of their own horses down on the camp, or creep up and suddenly scare the herd. Cattle are not affected in the same way. We have never heard of oxen or cows being liable to panic in darkness, unless from causes which would affect them equally in the daytime, such as the sight or smell of blood, or the sudden appearance of a herd of strange cattle near their feeding-ground.

As nearly all *wild* animals feed after sunset with an increased sense of security, and are then bold and confident where during the hours of daylight they are timid and suspicious, these terrors of the night among domesticated animals call for some special explanation. We can hardly assume that they have developed 'nerves' from artificial breeding and constant contact with man, except in the case of a few highly-bred dogs and horses; neither is there reason to believe that one species of ruminant animal is more averse to darkness than another. A probable explanation is that among all wild animals man is the chief object of fear, and as man cannot see in the dark, they gain a respite by night from their most besetting apprehension. The fear of carnivorous wild beasts is only secondary. But in the case of the domesticated animals the fear of man is exchanged for confidence, and wild beasts become their sole object of dread. In all countries where these are found, especially the wolf, the leopard, the lion, and the puma, the night becomes to domesticated animals a time of intense apprehension, having a definite object in some particular prowling beast. Darkness in itself is not the object of fear, but merely marks the time when the object of fear is abroad. Among our domesticated animals in this country the terror is not personified, but the nervousness survives in an impersonal form. It is not often in evidence, and needs some incident to arouse it; but there is no doubt that the propensity to fear increases with darkness and vanishes at daybreak.

The effect of darkness on insects shows some striking differences. Butterflies are so sensitive to want of light that they are not only stupid and sleepy at night, but are affected in the daytime by the shadow of every passing cloud. It is a common practice of butterfly-hunters to keep their eye on an insect without pursuing it, waiting till a cloud comes, when it is nearly certain to settle down and become more or less torpid. Possibly it fears rain; but some moths, whose wings are no less fragile than those of butterflies, often fly on evenings when a slight rain is falling. Except the owls and the night-jar, most of our night-feeding birds are thoroughly keen-sighted by day. They include the whole class of birds—ducks, waders, storks, and herons—which feed on the muds left by the tide. It is generally held that these birds can see equally well by night as by day. Very few people have spent enough time out on the muds by night to speak on this point with certainty; but a fowler who has had forty years' experience of night-shooting on the marshes, quoted in the *Badminton Magazine* some time ago, gives it as his opinion that all wildfowl see distinctly by night, but that, on the other hand, they do not recognise objects which they do not expect to see. They see and avoid a man walking, but if he is still they apparently mistake him for a piece of wreck or débris. Thus, when sitting in 'duck holes,' with the moon nine days old, he has known a pair of stints settle on the bank of the hole, and once caught one with his hand. He has also known an owl to fly into the hole and perch on the marram-grass with which it was lined; while another gunner declares that as he lay on his back on the shingle one night a mallard pitched between his feet and began to preen its feathers! The more familiar an observer grows with the ways of animals after dark and in the very early morning, the more convinced he is likely to become that they have made it an axiom that man is, or ought to be, in bed from dusk till six o'clock, and that even if he is not, the world during the hours of darkness and dawn belongs to them alone.

XXI.—NATURAL DEATH IN THE ANIMAL WORLD

Mr. F. G. AFLALO, in the *St. James's Gazette*, suggested that if death by accident is comparatively rare among animals, those which die a natural death meet it in the form of starvation. It is difficult to avoid the conclusion that wild animals, enfeebled by weakness or physical decay, do so perish, because of the absence of aid in sickness. If the bills of mortality from causes other than the violence of predatory species could be made out for the animal world, there would probably be good ground for the conclusion that this lingering death is in store for the majority.

The subject is complicated by a kind of mystery which has been long recognised in common experience, and is now attracting some of the attention it deserves from travellers and naturalists—the disappearance, namely, of the animal dead, other than those killed by accident or violence. In tropical countries rapid decay dissolves the tissues of flesh, and bone-devouring beasts like the hyæna may destroy the largest bones. But there is one region in which we should expect to find the bodies of such animals as have died a natural death, along the whole length of the frozen rim of the Old World, from the Petchora to Behring Sea, a region where even the fruits forced into being by the Arctic summer are preserved fresh beneath the snow until the ensuing spring, and the remains of prehistoric beasts, the mammoth and Siberian rhinoceros, have only undergone partial decay in the frozen soil. Here we should also expect to discover the bodies of animals which had died at the end of the summer 'cold-stored' till the snow broke up in the Arctic spring.

For this life during the Arctic summer is numbered by *millions;* there is probably no such gathering of birds on any part of the globe as on the Arctic tundra in July and August, while large and small mammals, seals, walrus, reindeer, foxes, and lemmings also abound. Do they never die, or what becomes of their bodies? For the latter are almost never seen. Nordenskiold, in his 'Voyage of the *Vega*,' more than once recurs to this strange absence of the animal dead. In an ice-beset channel among some Arctic islands off the mouth of the Yenesei he saw a great number of dead fish—*Gadus polaris*—and next day saw the sea-bottom, where the water was very clear, bestrewn with 'innumerable fish' of the same species, which had probably met their death by the shoal being enclosed by ice in a small hole, where the water could not receive a fresh supply of oxygen. This is a common form of natural death among fish in cold countries; but the explorer remarks it for the following reasons. 'I mention this,' he observes, 'because such examples of "self-dead" vertebrate animals are found exceedingly seldom. They therefore deserve to be noted. . . . During my nine expeditions in the Arctic regions, where Arctic life during the summer is so exceedingly abundant, the case just mentioned has been one of the few in which I have found remains of modern vertebrate animals which could be proved to have died a natural death. Near the hunting grounds there are often to be seen the remains of reindeer, seals, foxes, or birds that have died from gunshot wounds, but no "self-dead" Polar bear, seal, walrus, white whale, fox, lemming, or other vertebrate. The Polar bear and the reindeer are found there in hundreds; the seal, walrus, and white whale in thousands, and birds in millions. These birds must die a "natural death" in untold numbers. What becomes of their bodies?' Of this we have at present no idea; and yet we have here a problem of immense importance for the answering of a large number of questions concerning the formation of fossil-bearing strata. It is strange in any case that on Spitzbergen it is easier to find the vertebræ of a gigantic lizard of the Trias than the bones of a seal, walrus, or bird which has met a natural death.

This disappearance of the dead, so remarkable in itself, must, we think, be left out of account in the endeavour to ascertain the causes of decease. These must be sought, not by coroner's inquest, when too often there is no body which the jury can view, but by argument from the known causes of death among domestic animals, and the numerous, if scattered, records of mortality among wild ones, notes of which have often been carefully preserved, and may be found at intervals through the history of the last ten centuries. Most of these are the records of epidemics, but these and similar diseases must be held to be at work from year's end to year's end, even when not so violent as to cause remark; while concurrently there are among animals a large class of ailments causing natural death exactly analogous to those leading to human mortality.

Among these normal, non-epidemic causes of death many must be common both to wild and to domesticated species. 'Distemper' among dogs and cats probably extends also to foxes, wolves, and the wild felidæ. Its course is often exactly like that of a wasting low-fever, and animals die from it in precisely the same way as a human patient suffering from malaria or bilious fever, for the symptoms are not always the same. 'Chill' kills dogs, often by jaundice, and horses and cows mainly by causing internal inflammation. Death is then rapid and painful, and takes place before emaciation of any kind is visible in the animal. Most domesticated animals, even cage-birds, are liable to this cause of death; but we may assume that among wild animals whose normal course of life does not expose them to over-exertion or 'draughts' it is less common. Among aged domesticated animals, or those which are obliged to make violent exertions, heart-disease often causes sudden death. Master Magrath died from this, so do the racing dogs of the Northumberland miners. Aged horses sometimes drop down dead from the same cause when being gently ridden. Most very old horses which have been turned out to grass to end their days in peace suffer in the end from forms of indigestion, which cause them to become so thin that their owners order them to be shot. A recent veterinary work ascribes this and many other equine maladies to decay or defects in the teeth due to age or accidents. In the same way some old dogs become emaciated, even when carefully fed. But, like human beings, all the canine race, and most of the felidæ and bears, seem liable to forms of tumour, and unless relieved by surgery or released by euthanasia, may meet their death after great misery and suffering. Nor should it be forgotten that virulent sore throat is often prevalent and fatal amongst animals, especially cats.

Consumption and other forms of tuberculosis account for a large percentage of the natural deaths of domesticated animals. We doubt if any but the goat have complete immunity from it. Cattle, cats, chickens, pigeons, and in a less degree horses, dogs, rats, and mice, are all victims of the tubercle-bacillus. Between these normal and non-contagious causes of death and the violent and devastating animal plagues comes the long list of contagious animal diseases *mainly* confined to domesticated animals. Anthrax, the most rapid and deadly, is perhaps the least common. Then follows the permanent list—influenza, now always present and often epidemic, and affecting all domestic animals, and probably wild ones also ; swine fever, aphthous fever (not commonly fatal), glanders, and in some seasons the fatal 'liver rot,' mainly affecting sheep and rabbits, due to a parasite harboured in tainted ground and water. Add to these the choleraic diseases from bad water and dirty soil, and we have forms of natural death sufficient to account for the total disappearance of whole species, did not the generally healthy conditions under which they live act as a safeguard. Unfortunately, among these conditions is one which does not make for the preservation of health, namely, the tendency of nearly all non-carnivorous animals to herd together, and, even when non-related, to seek each other's society. Hence the astonishing violence and fatal results of animal epidemics. During their prevalence the absence of the animal dead is no longer marked. On the contrary, the bodies are in evidence. Among the multitude of examples collected by Mr. George Fleming in his work on 'Animal Plagues' are eighty-six epidemics affecting wild quadrupeds and birds, and twenty-seven affecting fish. Among the former nearly every wild species in Europe is mentioned, and some in the New World, including red-deer, reindeer, wolves, foxes, pelicans, bears, chamois, hares, wild hogs, rabbits, rats, wild-ducks, rooks, gaurs, and monkeys. Disorders usually somewhat rare and sporadic are capable of developing into epidemics and claiming victims wholesale. Perhaps one of the most curious instances is that of rabies among foxes. This prevailed on the Continent during the years 1830 to 1838. In the Canton of the Vaud in Switzerland the bodies of the dead foxes were often picked up and examined, and it was thought that they were suffering from malignant quinsy ; but as they entered villages and bit men, dogs, and swine, which afterwards died from rabies, there was no doubt as to the nature of the malady. In Wurtemburg and Baden the fox-rabies became so serious that regular hunts were organized until the animals were killed off, like the dogs of Lima under similar conditions. The effect of epidemics among animals is now so well known that we have dwelt in these remarks mainly on the less striking but still constant causes of natural death. But to those which perish in this normal course of mortality there must be added a vast number of wild animals which escape constitutional or contagious disorders, and die of lingering starvation, hastened by exposure. This fact in a great degree justifies the domestication and appropriation of animals to the service of civilized man, who in his dealings with their last years shows an ever-increasing tendency to rectify this aberrant conclusion set by Nature to animal life.

XXII.—ANIMALS' ILLUSIONS

A CURIOUS instance of animal illusion was seen on the Thames last summer by those on their way to Henley by river. A cock swan was fighting his own reflection seen in the window of a partly-sunken house-boat, which acted as a looking-glass. He had been doing battle for some time in defence, as he supposed, of his wife and family, who were grouped together close by, and had apparently begun to have some misgivings as to whether the enemy were real or not, for at intervals he desisted from the attack, and tapped the frame of the window all round with his bill.

Birds are perhaps more commonly the victims of illusions than other animals, their stupidity about their eggs being quite remarkable. Recently, for instance, a hen got into the pavilion of a ladies' golf-club, and began to sit in a corner on a golf-ball, for which it made a nest with a couple of pocket-handkerchiefs. But many quadrupeds are not only deceived for the moment by reflections, shadows and such unrealities, but often seem victims to illusions largely developed by the imagination. The horse, for instance, is one of the bravest of animals when face to face with dangers which it can understand, such as the charge of an elephant, or a wild boar at bay. Yet the courageous and devoted horse, so steadfast against the dangers he knows, is a prey to a hundred terrors of the imagination due to illusions—mainly those of sight, for shying, the minor effect of these illusions, and 'bolting,' in which panic gains complete possession of his soul, are caused as a rule by mistakes as to what the horse sees, and not by misinterpretation of what he hears. It is noticed, for instance, that many horses which shy usually start away from objects on one side more frequently than from objects on the other. This is probably due to defects in the vision of one or other eye. In nearly all cases of shying the horse takes fright at some unfamiliar object, though this is commonly quite harmless, such as a wheelbarrow upside down, a freshly felled log, or a piece of paper rolling before the wind. This instantly becomes an 'illusion,' is interpreted as something else, and it is a curious question in equine neuropathy to know *what* it is that the horse figures these harmless objects to be. One conclusion is certain: all horses share the feeling, *omne ignotum pro mirabili*, with a strong tendency to convert *mirabili* into *terribili*, and night or twilight predisposes them to this nervous condition. A coachman, who for many years had been in charge of a large stable of valuable carriage-horses, gave the writer some curious instances of the nervous illusions of horses. Once only did he find a whole stable in anything like permanent fear. He had taken ten carriage-horses to a large house in Norfolk, where they stood in a line in a ten-stalled stable. There was a tame monkey in the stable, very quiet, which slept unchained, sitting on one of the divisions of the stalls. On the first night, about eleven o'clock, he heard a disturbance in the stable, the horses stamping and kicking, and very uneasy. He got a light, entered the stable, and found them all 'in a muck sweat.' Nothing which could disturb them was there except the monkey, apparently asleep on its perch. He quieted the horses, locked the door, and went away. Soon the disturbance began again, and this time, slipping quietly up, he drew a pair of steps to one of the windows, and, as the moon was shining bright, had a view of the interior. The monkey was the source of terror. It was amusing itself by a steeplechase along the whole length of the stable, leaping alternately from the division of the stall to a horse's back or head, then off on to the next rail, and so on. The horses were trembling with fright, though many of them had not the least objection to a cat or a pigeon sitting on their backs. Yet the monkey had not hurt any of them, and their panic was clearly the result of illusion. Old-fashioned people used to identify any strange living object which frightened them with 'the devil.' Perhaps for horses 'the devil' is anything which they cannot understand.

'Understanding,' or investigation to that end, does often remove these equine illusions. Young horses can be led up to a sack lying on the ground and induced to pass it by letting them *smell* it, and find out that it really is a sack, and not the Protean thing, whatever it may be, which illusion conjures up for them. Once the writer saw a very quick and pretty instance of experiment by touch made by a frightened pony. It was being driven as leader in a pony tandem, and stopped short in front of where the rails of a steam-tramway crossed the road. It first smelt the near rail, and then quickly gave it two taps with its hoof. After this it was satisfied, and crossed the line. On the other hand, a donkey always tried to jump the shadows of tree-trunks on the road, though a similar experiment of touch would have shown that these were as unreal as the tram-rail was substantial. Lastly, no horse which has once knocked its head against the top of a stable doorway seems quite able to get rid of the illusion that there sits up in the top of all doorways an invisible something which will hit him again next time he goes through. Hence the troublesome, and sometimes incurable, habit of horses 'jibbing' at any doorway they may be required to go through. This is an obvious instance of the disadvantage at which most animals stand in regard to means of physical experiments. The horse, for instance, need only *feel* the lintel to find out that it is fixed and does not move, and is not alive and waiting to hit him. But, except his lips, which are sensitive, he has no member with which he can make this experiment. Except the elephant and the monkey, most of the 'higher' animals suffer from this lack of the means of experiment. The wonder is not that they suffer from illusions, but that they make so few mistakes.

The routine of chemical experiment gives some idea of the common means by which we guard against mistaking one thing for another. The inquirer notes the taste, scent and colour, and judges of the weight, solubility, and, in the case of crystals, of the shape of the object he wishes to identify; he tries if it is brittle or tough, he heats it or cools it. In common everyday experience the number of 'tests' unconsciously applied by men to prevent illusion and identify objects approaches much more nearly to the number prescribed for scientific inquiry than to the simple experiments used by animals. There is even a test for a ghost, which, since quoting Latin to it fell into disuse, usually takes the form of seeing if it is 'sensitive to percussion.' Now, even this simple experiment is denied to a horse when uncertain as to the reality of a figure seen by twilight. In the absence of a hand, the sense of touch is deficient in most animals. This deficiency, except in the case of birds, is not compensated by special acuteness of sight, though nearly all animals apply a sensible test to ascertain whether an object is living or inanimate. They wait to see if it moves; and to do this they know that the first condition is to keep absolutely still themselves. Most of the larger birds, notably woodpigeons, remain perfectly motionless for many seconds after alighting in a new place, in order to identify any moving object. On the other hand, the power of scent is a great corrective to animal misconceptions about objects. It is their chief means of distinguishing the animate from the inanimate, and is always employed by them in the diagnosis of *death*. It would be interesting to know whether camels and horses share the illusions produced on men by mirage in the desert, or whether they are all the time aware that the seeming lakes of water are unreal. It is certain that they are frequently mistaken in sounds, for there are many authenticated instances in which animals have mistaken the mimicry of parrots for the call of their masters, and a nervous dog, which had a special dread of thunder, has been known to go into a fit when it heard a sack of coals being emptied into the cellar.

XXIII.—ANIMAL ANTIPATHIES

A CORRESPONDENT describes a curious scene witnessed at the Zoological Gardens. He had for companion a gentleman, now dead, who was a dwarf, and walked with crutches. 'As soon as the tiger saw him he lashed his tail, and finally stood up on his hind-legs against the bars, and remained in a state of great excitement. We who saw it at the time were much struck by the sight, though whether its behaviour were due to alarm or intense curiosity we could not tell.' Probably the tiger's excitement was due to neither, but to the latent antipathy which many animals feel for anything abnormal, either in their own species, or even among others with which they are well acquainted. It is the feeling which prompts storks or rooks to destroy at once the young of other birds which are hatched from eggs placed in their nests, and dogs to bark at cripples or ragged beggars, or, as in this case, roused the dislike of an observant Zoo tiger, which saw men of normal size and proportions pass every day before its cage.

The belief in permanent antipathies among animals is very ancient. It appears in all the monkish bestiaries. There the otter is always the enemy of the crocodile, and the unicorn of the elephant;* while the dragon is hated by the hart, and in turn dislikes all beasts, including the panther, whose exquisite perfume, so agreeable to all other animals, disgusts the dragon, who runs away the moment he smells it. Turning from legend to facts, we find that animal antipathies have a range as wide or wider than the instinctive dislikes of men. They are in part exactly the same in kind as the latter, one animal exciting in another exactly the same disgust that a baboon or a blackbeetle does in the minds of many human beings; but the list of hereditary enemies—of one species which is the sworn foe of another, and has left in the weaker species an inbred and ancient sense of horror and fear—is far longer than the list of hereditary enemies of the dominant species, man. Instances of purely instinctive, inexplicable antipathy are naturally the least common, but there are very marked and definite examples. It is quite impossible, for instance, to account for the intense disgust which the camel excites in horses. They have

* Possibly this tradition is founded on the enmity which does really exist between the rhinosceros and the elephant.

been associated in many countries for centuries in the common service of man, and early training makes the horse acquiesce in the proximity of the creature which disgusts him. Otherwise it is far more difficult to accustom horses to work with camels than with elephants, precisely because the repugnance is a natural antipathy, and not a reasoned fear. They get used to the sight of an elephant, but the smell of a camel disgusts and frightens them. English horses which have never seen a camel refuse to approach ground where they have stood. Recently a travelling menagerie was refused leave to encamp on a village green in Suffolk, not because it was not welcome, for a wild-beast show is always vastly popular, but because the green was also the site of a market, and the farmers' gig-horses invariably refused to be driven across it after camels had stood there. Two bears were being exhibited in Harley Street recently, and no horse showed any fear of them. One horse almost touched the larger bear, but neither it nor the team of a four-in-hand which passed showed any nervousness.

Near relationship is no guarantee that instinctive antipathy shall not exist between two species. Hounds always hunt a fox, or in Brittany the wolf, with their hair standing up, though the same species of hound hunts deer or hares indifferently with the coat smooth. The innate dislike of bees for some persons is probably rightly attributed to some difference of scent, but why they dislike the scent of some people and like that of others, when both are equally well-disposed to the bees, is not known. It seems due to unreasoning caprice, to antipathy, and nothing else. The dislikes of dogs and cats for certain people are probably more reasonable. They divine, like children, who are really in sympathy with them and who are not ; neither is this a very difficult task, for most people are far more demonstrative with animals than they are when desirous of conciliating their own species.

From these antipathies of sentiment the antipathies of inheritance must be carefully distinguished. Many of these can be explained, though the motive is less obvious in some cases than in others. The hatred of all cattle for dogs is very marked. There is no doubt that this is a lasting inheritance from the days in which their calves were constantly killed by wolves or wild dogs. In India instances of sportsmen seeing the new-born calf, with its mother defending it from wolves, occur in most books on jungle sport, and the hatred of the *canidæ* associated with the strongest animal instinct, the love of their young, has never been effaced among cattle even in England, where the last wolf was killed in the days of Henry VII. Why the horse not only does not share this antipathy, but, on the contrary, loves a dog, it is difficult to explain. Wolves are very destructive to foals in Russia, especially in the Baltic provinces, where horse-breeding is an extensive industry. Possibly our English horses are mainly descended from the stable-bred animals imported after the disappearance of the wolf, and the ancestral fear of the *canidæ* has been eliminated.

Donkeys dislike dogs even more than cattle do, and, if loose, seldom lose a chance of kicking or biting them. The writer has seen a donkey chase a half-grown puppy into a stream, follow it in, and strike at it with its forefeet. It is now believed that the 'cat and dog' antipathy, which has passed into proverb, has also its origin in the destruction of the whelps of some of the large *felidæ* by wild dogs. There is much probability in this conjecture, for it is the dog, and not the wolf, which the tiger so intensely dislikes; and it is only the packs of wild dogs, and not wolves, which would venture to kill a cub. Leopards, which naturally live in the branches of trees, simply look on dogs as a favourite article of food, and the puma of the pampas, which inhabits a country where the wild dog is unknown, is also a great dog-killer. The dogs on their part seem quite aware of this difference of view on the part of the various cats; they will mob a tiger and hunt all tiger-cats; but they all seem to fear the leopard, and by nature to fear the puma, though in North America they can be trained to hunt it. It was recently noticed that a large dog, which found its way to a point opposite the outdoor cages of the lion-house at the Zoo, crept underneath a seat as soon as the puma caught sight of it, and exhibited signs of the utmost nervousness and fear. Most of the keepers at the Zoo are agreed that those animals which exhibit marked likes or dislikes for visitors have the strongest possible antipathy to black men. Children they also dislike, but for the obvious reason that the children tease them. It has long been noticed that all the monkeys hate a negro; but the experiment was recently tried on a large scale, and the scope of animal antipathy for the dark-skinned races was found to extend far beyond the monkey-house. When Mr. Hagenbeck's Somalis were at the Crystal Palace, they were invited one Sunday to see the Zoo, whither they went, accompanied by Mr. Menzies, the African explorer and hunter, who had brought them from Somaliland. There was nothing to which the most sensitive European could object in the appearance of these free, half-Arab tribesmen, and much that was most attractive. They were straight and tall; they had high noses, fine eyes, white teeth, and a skin the colour of a not quite ripe black grape. They were strict Moslems, exquisitely cleanly, washing constantly, not only their limbs and bodies, but their teeth and hair. They dressed in the whitest of linen, and carried weapons of the brightest steel, spending their spare moments in polishing either these or their teeth. They did not smoke, they did not drink, and the large room in which some thirty of them slept was as sweet as a hayloft. When all this gallant company of dark men entered the lion-house, there was an uproar. The animals were furious; they roared with rage. The apes and monkeys were frightened and angry, the antelopes were alarmed, and even the phlegmatic wild cattle were excited. They recognised their natural enemies, the dark-skinned men who have hunted them for a thousand centuries in the jungles and the bush, and with whom their own parents did battle when they were captured and carried off captive in the Nubian deserts, and, like the Grecian ghosts at the sight of Æneas in the shades, they raised a war-cry, though the sound did not die in *their* throats. Animal antipathy is thus closely correlated with like emotions in man. It may be traced in all its variations from purely instinctive and physical distaste, the dislike for the camel felt by the horse being much on a par with that felt by a Southern white for a South American negro, to its rational climax in antipathy based on danger known to animals and men alike, and exhibited in the common and intense horror of the poisonous snake. A tame monkey has been known to drop down in a dead faint when suddenly confronted with a snake. This sounds almost too human; but fainting in sudden terror, though rare among animals, in which this form of panic more often causes paralysis of the limbs, is not confined to monkeys. Gray parrots, which are highly nervous birds, will drop from the perch, and lose consciousness under any strong impulse of fright.

XXIV.—ANIMAL KINDERGARTEN

A WRITER in the *Reading Mercury*, describing the games played by lambs, says: 'From one point of view animal life is very serious, and if they are to survive in the struggle they can ill afford to waste time in frivolities. Young creatures are all educated on the Kindergarten system, and their games, in which the parents often join, are mainly mimic warfare or pursuit. The antics of lambs when playing the game "I am the King of the Castle," are just those which would be performed, though with more dignity, by a ram confronting his antagonist, and confident of his power to hurl him into the abyss.' This extension of the Duke of Wellington's observation on public-school games to the sports of animals is not without probability; for the instinct with which most young animals are equipped is, as a rule, insufficient to ensure their safety, until education both by their parents and playfellows comes to the aid of inherited impulse.

Mr. W. H. Hudson, when living on the Pampas of

KITTENS' KINDERGARTEN.

La Plata, recorded some very interesting observations on the education of the young of animals common on the plains. The half-wild lambs of the pampas remain almost 'imbecile' for three days. They are not senseless and helpless like blind puppies, but are equipped with certain instincts which do not answer the purpose for which they were apparently intended. The instances which Mr. Hudson gives of the unsatisfactory working of instinct—which in these lambs is properly so called, for it is prior to education and experience—show how their existence, intended to benefit the young creature, may actually retard education in the animal Kindergarten. The pampas lamb has three instincts when born. One is to suck, the second to run after anything moving away from it, and the third to run away from anything advancing towards it. It is in the second and third of these impulses that instinct is of disservice to the lamb. 'If the mother turns round and approaches it, even from a very short distance, it will turn round and run from her in fear, and will not understand her voice when she bleats to it; at the same time it will confidently follow a dog, horse, or man moving from it. It is a very common experience to see a lamb start up from sleep and follow the rider, running close to the heels of the horse. This is distressing to a merciful man who cannot shake the little simpleton off; and if he rides on, no matter how fast, it will keep up with him or keep him in sight for half a mile or more, and never recover its dam. . . . I have seen a lamb, about two days old, start up from sleep, and at once make off in pursuit of a puff-ball about as big as a man's head, carried past it over the smooth turf by the wind.'

The uneducated instinct in the case of these lambs is of disservice in place of service. The 'following' impulse, obeyed without discrimination, makes them lose their mothers, and the same want of knowledge makes them shun the very creature whose advance they should most desire. The old sheep is therefore obliged to devote herself during the first week of her lamb's existence to 'unteaching' instinct and substituting sense, which she does mainly by convincing the lamb that she, and no other creature, is to be followed. This first lesson once learnt, the rest follows easily. The fawn of the common pampas deer is born equipped with instinct for concealment similar to that which the young plover has on leaving the egg. But it is at once educated by the doe to use this to the best advantage. She teaches it to improve upon the original instinct. 'When the doe with a fawn is approached by a horseman with dogs she stands perfectly motionless, gazing fixedly at the enemy, the fawn motionless at her side. Suddenly, as if by some signal, the fawn rushes away from her at utmost speed ; and going to a distance of from six hundred to one thousand yards, conceals itself in a bottom, or among the long grass, lying down very close, with the neck stretched out horizontally.' The doe remains still until the dogs approach near, when she runs off in the opposite direction to that taken by the fawn. These pampas deer, which are clever enough to teach their young thus early, exhibit another artifice which marks them as of a higher intelligence than other species of deer. They have improved upon the common device of enticing the dogs in another direction than that taken by their young, just as they have improved upon the instinct common to all young fawns of lying still for concealment. The pampas deer feign lameness in order to draw the dogs away, a trick common among birds, but not used, so far as the writer is aware, by any other quadruped.

Young birds' education, in this particular direction, begins literally *ab ovo*. The same observer noted that in three widely differing species the young, when chipping the shell, instantly ceased their strokes, and the cry with which this effort is accompanied, when the old bird uttered its warning note. This he considers to be 'a proof that the nestling has no instinctive knowledge of its enemies, but is taught to fear them by its parents.' But it may be urged that in this case the knowledge of the meaning of the parent's note is also instinctive; for the nestling cannot know or realize the identity of the parent. The instance which Mr. Hudson quotes of the distinction which nestling birds do make between their 'own language' and an unknown tongue, is still more confusing to the theorist, though most interesting as a fact. The young of the parasitical starling of North America, known as the 'cow-bird,' never learn the warning notes of their foster-parents. 'They will readily devour worms from the hand of man, even when the old (foster) birds are hovering above them and screaming their danger-notes, while their own young, if the parasite has allowed any to survive, are crouching down in the greatest fear.' But when grown up and associating with their own kind they become suspicious and shy like other wild birds. All the 'catching-and-killing' games practised by cats and kittens, puppies, weasels, fox-cubs, and other young carnivora are educational, as are the wild gallops indulged in by mares with well-grown foals; but no one has ever seen a cow try to educate her calf, and little pigs, like Mr. Sam Weller, are expected to educate themselves. But they also educate one another.

It will be noticed that all creatures which have large families, whether beasts or birds, have less trouble in rearing them than those which have only one or two young. Little pigs are weeks ahead of calves in intelligence, and the young partridge, with its dozen brothers and sisters, is far more teachable than the young eagle. There seems no doubt that the latter is taught to fly by its parents. A correspondent informs the writer that he has watched the old birds so engaged, and the young eagles reluctantly following them to a height. Specialized education in animals begins late. The beaver kitten's training does not begin until the autumn of the year in which it is born. The old beavers, which have moved up tributary streams into the woods, or roamed to the larger lakes during summer, then return to inspect their dam, and repair it for the winter. They then cut down a few trees, and dividing them into logs, roll them or tow them to the dam. The kittens meantime are put on to what in a workshop would be called a 'soft job.' They cut all the small branches and twigs into lengths, and do their share of light transport service. In the mud-patting and repairing of the dam the beaver kittens take their share, but there is little doubt that they do so because their elders are so engaged. It is a Kindergarten of the best kind, because mud-patting and stick-cutting are a great joy and solace to old beavers as well as young ones, and so instruction, pleasure, and business are all combined. Young otters, and probably also young water-rats, have to be taught to go into the water. According to the observations of Mr. Hart, the late head-keeper at the Zoo, the young otters born there did not enter the water for weeks, and even then their mother had to 'mind' them and fetch them out when she thought they had had enough of it. They swim naturally when once in the water, and this seems true of all animals, though quite recently a young retriever, bred on a dry and waterless district in the Downs, was found to be unable to swim. A stick was thrown into the Thames for it to fetch. It plunged in, but soon sunk, and though rescued was almost insensible.

But such instances of instinct in abeyance are rare. More commonly the instincts for self-help and self-protection are early developed, but need direction and discipline. Generally speaking, birds are the quickest to learn when young, as well as the best equipped with original instinct.

XXV.—THE RANGE OF ANIMAL DIET

LIEUTENANT PEARY, discussing the hardships of Arctic travel, refuses to admit that living on Esquimaux diet is any hardship at all. On the contrary, he holds that conformity to the food and habits of indigenous peoples is the safest course for an explorer, and that 'fat and lean' whale or seal, eaten raw in alternate bites, makes rather an appetizing meal in high latitudes. Most people would prefer to do their exploring within reach of the comforts of the *Fram's* store-cupboard, so feelingly described by Dr. Nansen. But the experience of Lieutenant Peary and his wife, like that of many Arctic travellers before them, is evidence that the human digestion can cope with a potent change of diet when the change of climate and temperature corresponds.

It is self-evident that in the case of different human races the greater the range of diet the better chance of survival accrues. The districts of India where the population will only eat rice are at a disadvantage in times of scarcity compared with others which affect no single food grain. Famine is much less common among 'omnivorous' races than among those which are almost parasitic on a single plant like the banana or the potato. In spite of prejudices, which even in this country would make the lower classes more willing to forego a portion of their weekly meat-supply than to eat rye-bread in place of the wheaten loaf, the tendency everywhere is to increase the range and variety of food.

Among animals the same tendency can be traced. It appears most noticeably in domesticated species, but it can be traced amongst those which are wild, and in regions where evidence of its force as a working law is given by the very small number of creatures now found which live on a single item of food. In the case of domesticated animals the range of diet is often extended by compulsory detainments in regions in which they are forced to endure the winter which otherwise they would have avoided by migration.

The northern range of the horse and ox now far exceeds the natural food-limit. The Shetland pony could always pick up a bare living, but the Iceland pony has during the winter absolutely no natural food-supply. A few are taken into the houses, but the greater number are turned loose by their owners, and have for sole support sea-weed and the heads of dried cod. The Norwegian cow, spending the winter inside the Arctic circle, was formerly fed largely on soup made out of boiled fishes' heads, and the diet seems to have agreed with it. If anyone doubts the capacity of extending their food-range possessed by grass-eating creatures like cattle and sheep, and the scarcely less graminivorous horse—which has, however, a strong tendency, inherited from some remote ancestor, to eat bark and shoots like a rhinoceros—he need only run over the list of modern cattle-foods. Since the days when the Irishman had not learnt to make hay, and all his cattle were consequently killed off by Elizabeth's soldiers in the low valleys to which they were driven for food in winter, the cow has added to her *menu* hay, ensilage, sweet and sour, turnips, beet, Indian corn, cocoa cake, cotton-seed cake, rape-seed cake, locust beans, sugar, and 'grains.' Besides these, she has learnt to eat and prefer cooked food served warm to raw food eaten cold, and before long will probably be taught to supplement her cabbage and grass with 'cow-biscuits,' specially prepared to increase her yield of butter.

Horses, though training best on hay and oats, now eat cooked food, a mixture of hay, bran, vegetables, and corn being steamed and served up in most of the great London stables; and the only domestic creature whose tendency to enlarge its food-range is discouraged is the pig, not because it is bad for the animal, but because we desire by limiting its choice of food to extend our own. For our own purposes we have induced the dog to become largely a vegetable feeder, greatly to the advantage of his health in confinement, and, by the substitution of the uniform 'dog-biscuit' for table-scraps or meat, have given him a mixture of meal and dates which is as agreeable to crack as a bone. Among the more highly organized creatures 'single-food' animals are scarce and growing scarcer. There is evidence that the mute swan once fed almost entirely on sub-aquatic grasses. At Abbotsbury, when the ice destroyed the grass growing at the bottom of the lagoon, the half-wild swans refused to touch any other food, and starved in hundreds. Now they have learnt to eat grain, just as the Thames swans have learnt to eat bread and the grain which falls from barges. Probably the Abbotsbury swans were the last of their species in England which were 'single-food' animals, and with their conversion the extension of the range of diet is completed.

Reindeer feed almost entirely on mosses and lichen. It is still matter for doubt whether they can be acclimatized in this country, though experiments are being made to that end. If they cannot, an extension of the species, even though in domestication, will be prevented by their limited food-range. The moose feeds entirely on the bark and twigs of trees. But this is partly due to the height of its forelegs and the shortness of its neck, which make it almost impossible for it to graze. When fed from a manger the moose takes readily to ordinary cattle-food. Seals were long considered to live wholly on fish. The supply is so varied as well as abundant, and the seals so active, that it might be thought that there was little to induce them to seek a change. Yet Mr. Trevor-Battye when on Kolguev watched a seal catching ducks with such persistence and success that there can be little doubt that the seal has extended its dietary from fish to fowl. Instances of the converse are the great fishing owls, which, being provided with an equipment equally suited for killing birds and small animals, are by preference catchers of fish. Instances of carnivora developing a concurrent taste for vegetable food are uncommon. The most curious instance the writer has known was that of a Scotch deerhound, which was so fond of peaches that it would stand on its hind-legs to pluck those it could not reach when standing on all fours. The Australian Colonies present the three most striking instances of the tendency to extend the food-range in the direction of flesh diet. The often-quoted case of the large New Zealand parrot which took to sheep-killing is the most striking. But the feral pigs of the Colony are said to be very destructive to young lambs, and in 1833 in Australia throughout a large district the sheep became not only carnivorous but cannibal. The sheep of the Murrumbidgee country became addicted to eating a salt-impregnated earth found on the runs, and after some time became thin and emaciated. They then attacked the new-born lambs, and devoured such numbers that in one flock only four hundred were left out of twelve hundred. Some of the squatters applied for leave from the Government to move to other runs not yet taken up. Even the shepherds were attacked by the sheep when rescuing the lambs, and their clothes bitten. This morbid derangement of the instincts of the sheep, which was noted on many runs in the district, was never satisfactorily accounted for, but was generally attributed to the eating of the salt-impregnated earth. Of English birds, one, generally regarded as feeding entirely on vegetables and grain, occasionally varies its diet by animal food. This is the tame pigeon, which has been noticed after rain to eat earth-worms on lawns as eagerly as a thrush. This addition to its usual food is probably due to the absence in the diet generally given to the birds of some element which pigeons find in the mixed seeds and leaves which they eat when wild.

The flesh-eating habits of modern rooks in the North of England and Scotland have recently been the subject of a chorus of complaints from game-preservers and farmers. The rooks are, however, largely the victims of circumstance. The decrease of arable land, during the cultivation of which they found abundance of animal food, has forced the rooks to find a substitute, and this comes to hand in the form of young rabbits, pheasants, and chickens. In the corn countries of the United States the sparrow grows yearly more dependent on grain, and less insectivorous than his European reputation justifies, and in this country two consecutive severe winters made the tits take to bird-killing with an aptitude that shocked their patrons in English gardens. Highly specialized forms, such as the ant-eaters, the moles, and the leaf-eating sloths, must also of necessity confine themselves to the food which they are 'by intention' adapted to consume. But even the woodpecker and the wryneck, with claws specially adapted for scaling tree-trunks, and a beak formed to quarry rotten wood, are constantly seen feeding on the ground, mainly engaged in ravaging anthills; and kingfishers, scarcely modified from the shape of those which hover over English streams, dart with equal precision on the butterflies and beetles of tropical woods. Judging by the scarcity of the 'single-food' creatures, and the low place in the scale which they occupy, extension of the range of diet is almost a necessary law of their survival. Ant-eaters, sloths, and caterpillars may confine themselves to one article of food; but the more intelligent animals, like the higher races of man, have learnt better. One almost wonders whether the excuse of the Congo tribe who brought no palm-wine to the Belgian officers was true. They alleged that the elephants had drunk it all.

XXVI.—DAINTIES OF ANIMAL DIET

THE well-informed persons who wrote to the papers on the nature and uses of the persimmon, after the Prince of Wales's horse of that name won the Derby, omitted to notice that the fruit is in immense request as one of the dainties of animal diet. 'Brer Rabbit' achieved not the least notable of his diplomatic triumphs by inducing the other animals to get him persimmons when they wanted them themselves; and in fact there is no other fruit, except perhaps the water-melon, which is in more general request both among birds and beasts.

The taste for dainties among animals takes rather unexpected forms. Many flesh-eating creatures, for example, select as delicacies some form of fruit, and take considerable trouble to gratify what is a taste for luxury rather than a necessity of diet. The Syrian foxes, 'the little foxes which spoil the grapes,' are not the only creatures of their tribe which go for food to the vineyards. Jackals do the same, and eat the fruit not only as a luxury, but as a medicine. The 'grape cure' makes a marked difference in their condition, and animals which enter the vineyards suffering from mange are said to be restored to health very soon after their diet of grapes has begun. One British carnivorous animal, the marten, also seeks fruit as a dainty. In Sutherlandshire Mr. St. John discovered that some animal was stealing his raspberries, and, setting a trap, caught in it a marten cub. Dogs will also eat fruit, though rarely. When they do they usually take a fancy to gooseberries; the present writer has met with two spaniels which had this taste, and would take the gooseberries from the trees, and put out the skins after eating the pulp.

In the annual report on the management of the menagerie of the Zoological Society, the item 'onions' always figures largely in the bill for provender. Onions, as is well known to housekeepers, are an indispensable ingredient in very many dishes in which their presence is hardly recognised by those who would at once detect the presence of the smallest morsel of the vegetable if uncooked; and by most out-of-door populations, especially Spaniards and Portuguese, they are eaten raw with bread as part of their staple food. But no English animal seems particularly fond of them, and it is not easy to guess for whose benefit they are in such request at the Zoo. They are bought mainly for the

African antelopes and giraffes. All of the former, from the big roan antelopes to the miniature gazelles, 'dote' on onions, and regard them as the greatest delicacy which can be offered for their acceptance. It is said by trainers that if a horse once becomes fond of sugar he can be taught any trick for the circus. Antelopes could probably be trained in the same way by rewards of onions. There is one drawback to their indulgence in this dainty, which leads to some restriction of its use at the Zoo. After an onion-breakfast the scent in the antelope-house, usually redolent of odorous hay and clover, is overpowering, and visitors who do not notice the fragments of onion-tops upon the floor are inclined to leave in haste, and class the antelopes among the other evil-smelling beasts of the menagerie. For the giraffes they were not only a *bonne bouche*, but also a very wholesome change in their ordinary food, and though the liking for the bulb is an acquired taste—for onions are not native to the South African veldt—the new giraffe is as fond of them as its predecessors. Deer show no particular preference for onions; on the other hand, they prefer apples to any other dainty. In the Highlands the wild deer have no chance of invading an orchard; but on Exmoor and on the Quantock Hills, where they have now greatly increased in numbers, they leave the hillsides and thick plantations and rob orchards by moonlight. The stags thrust their horns among the apple-boughs and shake off the fruit, and even leap up to strike the branches which are beyond their reach when standing. In enclosed parks red-deer find a substitute for apples in the small unripe horse-chestnuts which fall in dry weather. At the Sheen Lodge of Richmond Park, near which several chestnut-trees stand, the stags have been known to slip out through the gate to pick up the fallen fruit lying on the road. Fallow-deer seem less fond of fruit than the red-deer. Bread is the delicacy by which they are most easily tempted, though, except in such small enclosed parks as that of Magdalen College at Oxford, they are rarely tame enough to take it from the hand. At Bushey Park, where the herbage is unusually rich, and the fallow-deer fatten more quickly than in any of the royal parks, there is one old buck who has acquired such a taste for bread that he has left the main herd, and established himself as a regular beggar near the Hampton Court Gate. The benches between this gate and the circular pond and fountain near the head of the great avenue are naturally favourite seats for Londoners who come down and bring their luncheon with them. The moment the buck sees a couple comfortably seated and a paper parcel produced and opened, he sidles up, and gazes with all the expression of which his fine eyes are capable at the buns and bread-and-butter. If a piece be held out to him, he walks up, and stretching forward as far as he can without overbalancing, takes it from the hand. At this moment his dignity and grace somewhat decline, for his excitement is such that he curls his tail over his back, and looks like a terrier.

Hares, like most rodents, do not show strong preferences in their choice of food, the chief 'preference' being that there shall be plenty of it, and that it shall be green and tender. But they will come great distances to feed on carrots. Some Devonshire magistrates recently refused to convict a person charged with poaching a hare, on the ground that they, as sportsmen, did not believe that there was a hare in the parish in which the offence was alleged to have been committed. The facts rather favoured this view, but the planting of a field of carrots in this hareless area soon attracted the animals. Rabbits, which are by common consent able to get a living where no other quadruped can, become very select in their tastes where food is abundant, and soon seek variety. In the gardens of a large house in Suffolk, adjoining a park in which rabbits swarmed before the passing of the Ground Game Act, it was found that some rabbits managed to effect an entrance every night, with a view to eating certain flowers. These were clove-pinks and verbenas. No other flowers were touched, but the pinks were nipped off when they flowered, and the verbena plants devoured as soon as they were bedded out. Farmers have lately been advised to try feeding their stock upon sugar, which is both cheap and fattening. This would be good hearing for many horses, which like nothing so well as lump-sugar; but neither cows nor pigs seem to be particularly fond of sweetstuff in this form, though the latter are very partial to raw, crushed sugar-cane. But the pig, though greedy and omnivorous when kept in a sty, and a very foul feeder on the New Zealand runs, is most particular in its choice of food when running wild in English woods. Its special dainties are underground roots and tubers, and it is the only animal, except man, which appreciates and seeks for the truffle. For all these underground delicacies its scent is exquisitely keen. If by any mishap a pig enters a garden at the time when bulbs are planted, it will plough up a row of snowdrops or crocus-roots, following the line as readily as if they lay exposed to the surface. On the other hand, pigs seem to have discovered that raw potatoes are unwholesome. Cooked potatoes are devoured greedily; but the raw tuber is as a rule rejected, unless the animal is very hungry, and though pigs will sometimes root among the potato-mounds, it is in search of other food than potatoes. Stud-grooms have decided that carrots are the favourite dainty of the horse, and accordingly it has become part, in many stables, of the under-groom's duty to slice carrots and arrange them on a plate ready for the master or mistress to take to the horses when visiting them. They like apples equally well, but these do not always agree with them. There is, or was recently, at Guildford Station a horse which would push a truck with its chest, when told to do so, instead of pulling it. This was very useful when it was desired to bring the truck up to the end of a siding, where there was no room for the horse to go in front and pull. It had been taught by a shunter, who sat in an empty truck and offered the horse a carrot. The horse would stretch its neck out, and push its chest against the waggon to take the carrot, and so start the waggon along the metals. It was then given the carrot, and soon learnt that it was wanted to push and would be rewarded for doing so.

Donkeys are said to *like* thistles. They will eat them, and will even take them from the hand and eat them when other food is at hand. But they do not exhibit much enthusiasm for this dainty, and would probably agree with Bottom that 'good hay, sweet hay, hath no fellow.' Camels, however, really enjoy them, and menagerie camels when on tour will eat every thistle they can pick by the roadside. This is a curious taste in daintiness, but, like some human fancies of the kind, it has a sentimental background. The camel, it is said, eats the thistles because they are the nearest approach to the ' vegetation ' of its native desert.

XXVII.—THE SLEEPING HOMES OF ANIMALS

As animals' beds are almost the only pieces of furniture which they construct, so their sleeping-places or bedrooms represent most nearly their notion of 'home.' The place selected to pass the hours of sleep, whether by night or day, is more often than not devoid of any efforts at construction. It is chosen for some qualities which strike the owner as suitable for rest and quiet, and from that moment it arouses in the animal mind some part of the human sentiment which we know as 'the love of home.' This association of ideas with their sleeping-places is entirely distinct from the so-called 'homing instinct,' or sense of direction. It is a sentiment, not a mental process, and is exhibited by creatures which are not commonly credited with memory or the power of thought. Some butterflies, for example, return regularly to the same place to sleep, and their proverbial flightiness does not prevent them from entertaining the sentiment of home. The first vindication of butterfly memory was occasioned by the regularity with which a small butterfly named *Precis Iphita* returned to sleep in a veranda of a musical club at Manghasar, in the Dutch East India Islands. Mr. C. Piepers, a member of the Dutch Entomological Society, noticed that this butterfly returned to the same place on the ceiling during the evening. In the day it was absent, but at nightfall, in spite of the brilliant illumination of the veranda, it was again sleeping in the same spot. ' It was not to be found in the daytime, being probably absent on business,' writes Mr. Piepers ; ' but as civilization has not advanced so far in Manghasar that it is there considered necessary to drive away every harmless creature which ventures into a human dwelling, I had the pleasure of admiring the memory of this butterfly for six consecutive nights. Then some accident probably befell it, for I never saw any trace of it again.'

It is difficult to imagine a spot with less domestic features to adorn the home than a piece of the bare ceiling of a tropical veranda ; but the attachment of animals to their chosen sleeping-place must rest on some preference quite clear to their own consciousness, though not evident to us. In some instances the ground of choice is intelligible. Many of the small blue British butterflies have grayish spotted backs to their wings. At night they fly regularly to sheltered corners on the chalk downs where they live, alight head downwards on the tops of the grasses which there flourish, and, closing and lowering their wings as far as possible, look exactly like a seed-head on the grasses. If the night is cold, they creep down the stem and sleep in shelter among the thick lower growth of grass. The habits of birds in regard to sleep are very unlike, some being extremely solicitous to be in bed in good time, while others are awake and about all night. But among the former the sleeping-place is the true home, the *domus et penetralia*. It has nothing necessarily in common with the nest, and birds, like some other animals and many human beings, often prefer complete isolation at this time. They want a bedroom to themselves. Sparrows, which appear to go to roost in companies, and sometimes do so, after a vast amount of talk and fuss, do not rest cuddled up against one another, like starlings or chickens, but have private holes and corners to sleep in. They are fond of sleeping in the sides of straw-ricks, but each sparrow has its own little hollow among the straws, just as each of a flock of sleeping larks makes its own 'cubicle' on the ground. A London sparrow for two years occupied a sleeping-home almost as bare of furniture as the ceiling which the East Indian butterfly frequented. It came every night in winter to sleep on a narrow ledge under the portico of a house in Onslow Square. Above was the bare whitewashed top of the portico, there were no cosy corners, and at eighteen inches from the sparrow was the gas-lit portico-lamp. There every evening it slept, and guests leaving the house seldom failed to look up and see the little bird fast asleep in its enormous white bedroom. Its regular return during two winters is evidence that it regarded this as its home; but why did it choose this particular portico in place of a hundred others in the same square?

It is a 'far cry' from South Kensington to the Southern cliffs; but the same sense of home which brought the sparrow back nightly to his London portico brings the cormorants and the falcons to the same spot in the same precipice, year after year, in the Culver Cliffs. There is a certain vaulted niche, in which the peregrine falcons sleep, winter and summer, in the white wall of the precipice, and every night at dusk the cormorants fly in to sleep on their special shelves and pedestals on another portion of the cliff. They come to these few square yards of perpendicular chalk, three hundred feet above the surge, as constantly as the fishermen return to their cottages at the Foreland. They regard this sleeping-place as their fixed and certain home, where, safe from gun, cragsman, or cliff-fox, they can sleep till sunrise sends them hungry to their business of fishing. But of all animal sleeping-places, caves and caverns are most remarkable for ancient and distinguished habitation. Like prehistoric man, the animals alike of past ages and of the present hour have made caves their bedrooms, and that they regard these in the light of home is almost certain, for they return to die there. Whether the last English rhinoceros slept in the Derbyshire cave where his bones were found can only be matter of conjecture. But caves are the natural sleeping-places of nearly all nocturnal creatures, which need by day protection from enemies and from the disturbing light. Hollow trees serve the smaller creatures; but the great caves, especially those of the tropical forest, whether on the Orinoco, or in Central America, or the Indian Archipelago, or in prehistoric Kentucky, have been the sleeping-places of millions of creatures from the remotest ages of the earth. There sleep the legions of the bats; there the 'dragons' and monsters of old dreamed evil dreams after undigested surfeits of marsupial prey or of prehistoric fish from vanished seas; and there the wolf, the bear, the panther, and the giant snake still sleep away the hours of day.

Other animals, in place of seeking and maintaining a private bedroom, prefer to sleep together in companies. Aristotle's remark that 'carefulness is least in that which is common to most' holds good of these communal sleeping-places. Even clever creatures like pigs and domestic ducks have no 'home' and no permanent sleeping-quarters. Like the Australian black, who, when presented with a house, pointed out the peculiar advantages offered by square buildings, because they always offered a wall to sleep against, *outside*, whichever way the wind blew, they have to shift their quarters according to the weather. With these limitations, pigs are extremely clever in choosing sleeping quarters. The wave of heat during the second week of August was preceded by two days of very low temperature and rain. In a row of model pigsties, during these cold days, nothing was visible but a large flat heap of straw in each. This straw was 'stuffed' with little pigs, all lying like sardines in a box, keeping each other warm, and perfectly invisible, with the straw for a blanket. Then came the heat, and some hundred swine were let loose in a paddock. By noon the whole herd were lying in the shadow of a large oak, every pig being fast asleep, close together in the shade circle. In another meadow two flocks of Ailesbury ducks were also fast asleep in the grass, in the shadow of the oaks. But social animals, which live in herds and often move considerable distances in search of their daily food, are known to resort to fixed sleeping-places on occasion. Among the wildest and least accessible creatures of the Old World are the wild sheep. Hunters in the Atlas Mountains commonly find chambers in the rocks which the aoudads, or Barbary wild sheep, use to sleep in.

Some are occupied by a single ram, others are used by small herds of five or six, or an old sheep with her lamb. The ovine scent so strong near domestic sheep-folds always clings to these rock chambers of the wild sheep. The 'big horn' of the Rocky Mountains is also found in holes in the hills, but these are believed to be made by the sheep eating salt-impregnated clay, until they burrow into the hill. They may be 'bolted' from these holes like rabbits. Even park deer sometimes occupy bedrooms. In one old deer park in Suffolk some of the giant trees show hollow, half-decayed roots above ground, like miniature caves. Into these the young deer used to creep in hot weather, when the flies were troublesome, and lie hidden and cool.

Fish, which not only need sleep like other creatures, but yawn when drowsy, and exhibit quite recognisable signs of somnolence, sometimes seek a quiet chamber to slumber in. This is obvious to any who will watch the behaviour of certain rock-haunting species at any good aquarium. The 'lump-suckers,' conger-eels, and rock-fish will retire into a cave in the grotto provided for them, and there go fast asleep; though as their eyes are open their 'exposition of sleep' is only proved by the absence of movement, and neglect of any food which comes in their reach. Their comparative safety from attack when asleep in open water may be due to the sensitiveness of their bodies to any movement in the water. But pike are easily snared when asleep, probably because, being the tyrants of the waters themselves, they have less of the 'sleeping senses' possessed by most animals which go in fear of their lives from hereditary enemies.

XXVIII.—THE CARRIAGE OF ANIMALS

MOST animals are so admirably equipped for transporting themselves on long journeys, whether by land, air, or water, that they have the greatest possible dislike to any artificial mode of conveyance, however carefully designed to meet their convenience. Collectors of rare animals in distant and savage countries find this question of transport a much more serious difficulty than either the capture or the feeding of the beasts when caught. If possible, they are so far tamed before the return expedition as to make it possible for them to accompany their captors, making use of their own legs as far as the rail or ship.

In South Africa, where the Boer hunters expect to make some profit from live animals as well as from meat and hides, zebras are always tamed before being despatched from the interior, and a number of these, with young antelopes of various species, may often be seen, half-domesticated, round the hunter's temporary camp. But there is a regular trade in certain classes of wild animals which could never be permitted any degree of liberty, owing to their temper or unmanageable dimensions. These are transported from immense distances before any 'civilized' means of transport is available. Mr. Hagenbeck informed the writer that he once brought, amongst other creatures, fifty lions and leopards, besides rhinoceroses, from the neighbourhood of the Atbara, or Black Nile, to the Red Sea coast, without losing one animal. The regions traversed were partly fertile and populated, but partly broken by strips of desert. The difficulty of transport was more apparent than real. Nearly all the animals were quite young, the lions being not more than a quarter grown. These, with the leopards and hyænas, were carried in cages made of hard native wood, with bars on one side only, exactly like cages in which birdcatchers carry linnets. These were slung on the backs of camels, with a thick pad between the back of the cage and the camel's flank. The only serious difficulty encountered was in the transport of the rhinoceroses. Though young, they were very bulky, heavy, and absolutely unmanageable. They were also very valuable, and it was decided to spare no pains to bring them safely to the coast. After some experiments, it was found possible to put each of the rhinoceroses in a kind of litter, slung on poles. These were laid across the backs of a pair of the strongest camels procurable, 'dray-horses of the desert,' of which several were taken with the Khalifa, and served by relays in the capacity of 'rickshaw' bearers to the black rhinoceros calves.

Before the days of railways, English animals, from geese to cattle, nearly always travelled on their own feet. Until they reached the towns this method was very agreeable to them, and they lost very little in condition. Before the Great Western Railway was made, there was a large trade in driving cattle from the Western counties to London. They were assembled at Bath, and as soon as possible were driven up on to the Downs, where they travelled along the 'green roads' until close to London. Horses are the only creatures for which decent accommodation is provided on our railways. In fifty years the railways have never yet risen to the occasion of providing even reasonably convenient transport for any other animals; of intelligent design, or appreciation of the difficulties in the way of accommodating creatures whose whole experience is foreign to the necessities of close packing or maintaining their balance when the surface on which they stand is in motion, there is no trace. That they may want food or water on a long journey, or even protection from the cold, did not apparently enter the minds of the early designers of 'cattle-trucks.' The abominable discomfort of the old third-class carriage designed for the use of human passengers is an indication of the ignorance and indifference of the early designers of 'rolling stock.' But the improvement in this department has been constant, though slow. A class of 'improved' cattle-vans has been introduced on some lines, but the supply is at present very scanty. As a rule, valuable animals are sent in a horse-van, at about the cost of a first-class passenger fare, with the risk of being 'jammed' by trying to turn in a compartment designed for an animal of different shape. A practical writer on cattle recommends that they shall be put in 'tail first,' to obviate this difficulty. But the bulk of British cattle travel by rail in open trucks, exposed to the violent draughts made by the train's movement, and to the inflammations of the eyes and nostrils set up by the constant rush of dust and particles of grit from the line. Sometimes a tarpaulin shelters them from sun and rain; but in all cases they go by 'goods train.' No owner of prize cattle would think of sending them by this, the general means of carriage. Telegrams from India during the late frontier rising spoke of camels loaded up on rail for service at the front being kept waiting in sidings for four days, and dying in the trucks. It would appear from this that there are no proper camel-vans yet provided on Indian railways. For the Government elephants admirable railway carriages are provided. They are built of steel, with a steel hood in front to protect the elephant from draught and dust. The rear of the truck is arched over with steel girders, and a double steel rail supports the elephant on either side. In some admirable illustrations of elephant life recently published, the process of 'entraining elephants by means of railway elephants trained to the business, who coax and push them on board,' is very clearly shown.

Dog-boxes! These survive, like the 'clink' and the stocks in old villages, in the designs of guard's vans; but for years no humane guard has ever used these carefully barred, dark little dungeons. At present there is no suitable accommodation whatever for dogs travelling by rail, except on the Scotch expresses. They are simply tied up among the parcels in the guard's van, an inconvenient and objectionable practice. Sheep suffer less than cattle on railway journeys. Being lower in the legs and addicted to huddling together, they are sheltered by the sides of the truck from the draught and dust, and keep each other warm. Prize rams and sheep travel in the guard's van, and often become quite experts at railway journeying. They jump in, lie down, and jump out with very little persuasion. One celebrated old ram who lives on the Great Western line, knows his own station and the porter who usually detrains him as well as a dog would, and when hailed by his railway friend, jumps up, gives himself a shake, and bounds out of the carriage on to the platform when released by the guard.

Pigs frequently die of chill after railway journeys in the open trucks. In place of these there should be special covered-in pig-vans. As pigs huddle close together, and take little room, the slight increase in cost of carriage would be more than compensated. Of all animals pigs are the most tiresome to 'carry' by any form of conveyance. Lifting a pig into a dealer's cart is one of the tragedies of village life. He is heavy, dirty, and active. He 'makes a stiff back' like a baby, his hoofs are sharp, he seems as muscular as a salmon, and his yells and screams are distracting. Custom insists that he shall be held and partly lifted by his tail. This adds to his resentment. When once up in the cart a net is fastened over him, and he usually settles down in such a position as to spoil the balance of the trap as far as possible. From the horse's point of view a pig is always the worst possible passenger. A celebrated Suffolk dealer, after lifting pigs for some twenty years into his cart, actually hit on the grand idea of having a low cart built, hanging within a couple of feet of the ground. Into this quite a small herd could be *driven*, not lifted, and he could stand up and drive it with the pigs wedged tight all round his legs. When a herd of lean pigs are destined for a journey by rail, the question of transfer from carts to truck is a serious one. They are often placed in a pig-yard in districts where there is much demand for their transport, and 'driven on board.' Recently the writer found the staff of a station on a Western line of railway dispersed in various directions up and down the line, equipped with lanterns, and in pursuit of seven pigs which had escaped from a truck. It is to the credit of the porters that all of the truants were caught except one, who met his death by collision with an 'up express.'

This incident may be compared with the adventures of a pedigree bull despatched early this summer to the Isle of Wight. The animal was shipped at Portsmouth in one of the small sailing boats which still play the part of carriers' vans between the mainland and the island. The bull was in charge of a man, who held it by a chain fastened to a ring in its nose. When half way across the Solent the chain broke, and the bull was loose in this open lugger, with four or five passengers, trusses of hay, luggage, potato-casks, and the rest of the assorted cargo. Fortunately, it was an imaginative bull; the man in charge fastened a piece of string to the ring, jerked it, and the bull, which was showing a disposition to walk about the boat, became submissive, under the impression that he was still chained.

Calves, lambs, turkeys and swans are usually carried by

rail or boat in crates. This is perhaps the most humane way of moving them, for they have not to be driven or handled. An axis-deer recently brought from France was enclosed in a large wooden case, with flat boarded bars. It smashed this, though its horns were sawn off, and got loose in the guard's van. Then it attacked the guard, who had to escape on the footboard and stop the train till the creature was secured. An Indian buffalo presented to the Zoological Society by a Rajah on a visit to this country was taken there in a parcel-post van with its head stretching out at the back. Birds are by no means so easy to carry securely as might be imagined. Pigeons often fight when confined in baskets, and birds for showing are sent in low hampers with V-shaped partitions, in each of which a pigeon is stowed away. Prize fowls are placed in tall open-work baskets, in which they can stand upright. Parrots are bad travellers. They generally seize the side of any box or basket in which they are placed with their beaks. This is in order to hold on when carried. Soon they rather like the sensation, and steadily eat a hole in their box. To avoid this a wooden perch should be fastened to the *bottom* of whatever receptacle they are placed in. Canaries and small birds are often carried in the large cages in which they live. This is a mistake. They are more comfortable and more easily carried in the small close cages which bird-catchers use when travelling.

Cats and all small animals should always travel in a hamper, with hay or flannel at the bottom and a lining of thick brown paper on the sides, though not covering the top. This prevents their seeing through the hamper and keeps them quiet, while it protects them from draughts when waiting on the station platforms.

XXIX.—TRESPASSING ANIMALS

At a Parish Council recently held to consider the Jubilee bonfires, it was suggested that there should also be a Jubilee restoration of the parish pound. It was successfully urged against this that, since the Inclosure Act, animals have ceased to trespass, and that the proposal was as retrograde as one to renew the parish stocks. This view is incorrect both in fact and theory; for enclosure really tempts to trespass, and the desire to do so is as deeply rooted in animal as in human nature. When people trespass in order to kill someone else's game, or to take apples, or birds' eggs, or flowers which do not belong to them, the act is naturally regarded with severity. But most human trespassing is done in order to enjoy nice places which are the property of other people, to luxuriate in open spaces instead of keeping to the road, and to gratify a lawless desire for æsthetic and physical expansion. Children trespass in order to run about and pick flowers; older people usually allege that 'they only wanted to look'

—which is partly true, and is in some degree an apology for intrusion. It is this which tempts people to invade the nice shady lawns of riverside houses; to stray off footpaths into the mowing grass; and to walk into cool college quads, where they imagine (wrongly) that they are trespassing. It even led to Mr. Pickwick being wheeled to the pound. There are those who say that the knowledge that the invader has no right to be there adds to the pleasure of trespass. We doubt it greatly. But we have no doubt at all that many animals are perfectly aware of the illegal side of trespass; that they know that it is naughty and disallowed, and that in doing so they are contravening the rights of property. This, of course, involves the supposition that animals understand property not only in things but land. There are many 'leading cases' to prove this, the commonest being the vigour with which dogs drive any strange animal out of their master's garden. Dogs are so well aware of the whole moral and legal aspects of trespass, that when once they have made up their minds to it they actually *trade on the knowledge* that their owner has a conscience, though they have not. We have noticed this in great perfection in the case of canine trespass on the grass circles in the front of a semi-public building in London. This delectable piece of grass is divided from the road by a high railing, but the gate usually stands open.

Dogs, passing with maids on their way to do shopping, or with children out for a walk, after some reconnoitring, dash in and have delightful games on these grass-plots, with rolling over, racing round, and general high jinks. The maids and children, being shy, and not liking to trespass, stand at the gate, call, whistle, and implore. But the dogs go on just the same. This is a common form of dog trespass. Its meaner side was painfully shown in the following case. Most well-brought-up small boys, who are naturally much tempted to trespass, are so lectured and frightened with stories of policemen that they are quite nervous on the subject. One such small boy, attended by a collie dog, was passing, when the dog ran in at the gate, and, being instantly joined by a friend, proceeded to race and play on the grass. The good little boy stood at the gate and whistled till the tears ran down his cheeks with anxiety. But his dog took not the slightest notice. He only played harder with his friend. At last the boy walked gingerly in on the path, and came up to the edge of the turf on which the dog was playing. To trespass further than that was more than the boy's conscience would permit; so he stood by the edge of this grass as if it were a pond of water too deep to venture into. The dog saw and took instant advantage of his scruples. He played on in his grass circle just as boldly as before, while the poor boy drifted round the edge, holding out his hand, calling, whistling, and imploring, but in vain. Then the door of a lodge opened, and a pitying porter came to the rescue. He had hardly stepped out of his lodge when the two dogs grasped the situation and bolted, leaving the boy to any fate which their wickedness had laid up for him.

Such shocking examples of animal law-breaking must not be confounded with the wish to obtain liberty which prompts donkeys to undo knots on gates with their teeth, or horses to open the latch of their stables with their lips and noses. Cats also invade all gardens and roofs at will; but that is because they feel they have a right to go where they please. Pigs, on the other hand, are inveterate trespassers from their earliest infancy. They inherit this from the wild pigs, which will travel many miles every night to explore new feeding-grounds, and return by dawn to their day-haunt. Little pigs trespass mainly from a spirit of adventure and inquiry. That is what makes it almost impossible to keep a litter of pigs anywhere near a country house. They organize trespassing parties, which grow bolder daily. One day they come round and look at the back-door. The next day one runs into the passage, and pokes his nose into the kitchen. In time they find some open door, and turn up unexpectedly on the tennis-lawn, or raid the bulbs in the crocus-beds. In the course of their travels they eat all they find which is edible, though this is an incident, not a motive, of their trespass. Here we must tell a story which should be added to the many moral tales for children of which good and bad pigs are the heroes. A litter of small pigs escaped from their yard by squeezing through the gap left by a broken paling. In the course of a delightful ramble they found much food, of which they ate immoderately. Being discovered, they fled for refuge to their sty; but their greediness had, for the time, so increased the girth of their bodies, that only the smallest could squeeze back again into the sty, and the rest, after making most painful efforts to do so, were obliged to remain outside. Older pigs trespass to obtain food, and are expert at breaking through fences; but their omnivorous taste in food makes them, as a rule, contented to roam round the farmyard and buildings. Cattle feeding entirely on grass are much given to raiding neighbouring fields in which the herbage is better than in their own, and, in addition, often trespass from some innate liking for the act. Their ingenuity and perseverance in effecting an entry to the ground they propose to trespass on is remarkable. They will wait for hours and watch a gate until someone passes through it, when they at once walk up and try it to see if the latch has been left unfastened. As might be expected, Irish cows have this 'land hunger' and trespassing instinct de-

A TRESPASSING PARTY. *From a drawing by Lancelot Speed.*

veloped in a high degree. We have seen little black Kerry cows go down on their knees—that being the first movement when a cow lies down, and therefore quite familiar to them as a means of 'stooping'—and literally *creep* under the chains suspended between a row of posts which divided them from a lawn on which they desired to walk. Bulls are even greater trespassers, though rougher in their methods. Some bulls always smash the gate of any field they are kept in. Others use gentler methods, and turn up in most unlikely places. A young bull and heifer in the Isle of Wight got out of a field, and were found together next morning in a ground-floor room of an empty house. This bull had a taste for midnight trespassing, and on one occasion found its way into a field, where it bellowed loudly. Its owner, thinking that a cow was ill, went with a lamp to see what was the matter. The lamp was extinguished with some haste when he discovered who the visitor was.

Trespass by birds sounds like a paradox, for it suggests an exclusive claim to the use of the air above the owner's property. As a fact, certain birds are inveterate and wilful trespassers, but they nearly always trespass *on foot*. The greatest offenders are ducks, geese, and guinea-fowls and chickens, all of which are quite aware, or very soon learn, when they are on forbidden ground, but are only too eager to go there

when there is anything to be got by it. A country
rector, on seeing his neighbour's ducks and a couple
of geese walking for the tenth day in succession
through his meadow-grass on their way to his straw-
berry-beds, remarked with resignation that he supposed
he must have a wooden fence put up. 'No, sir, no,'
replied his gardener bitterly; 'you aren't obliged to
keep no fence against *them things as flies.'* The force
of this remark on the futility of building a wall to
keep out birds was unanswerable, and sounded like the
basis of natural law as to bird trespass. Instances in
which animals recognise or maintain rights to certain
ground against other animals are not common. A dog
will turn trespassing cattle out of his master's corn
without orders, but he seldom asserts a personal right
to more than his own bed or kennel. This he defends
vigorously. The keenness with which the Constan-
tinople street-dogs reserve their own particular quarter,
sometimes limited by an arbitrary boundary, such as
the centre of a street, one side of which belongs to one
set of dogs, and another to another, is an instance to
the contrary. But, except in the case of the large
carnivora, both beasts and birds, there is little disposition to assert a right to definite areas, and 'carefulness being least in that which is common to most,'
there can be no resentment of trespass where there is
no feeling for property.

XXX.—DO ANIMALS TALK?

IF animals talk, as we are convinced that they do, to the limited extent of conveying wishes or facts by sounds, their speech ought to conform to the divisions of human speech. There must, in fact, be an 'animal grammar,' in the terms of which they express themselves. It is no bad test of the assertion that animal speech exists to apply the old formal divisions of the grammarians to the instances in which they appear to 'voice' their thoughts, and ascertain by trial whether the forms into which the human speech has been divided fit the latter. The time-honoured divisions of speech are (1) statement of fact; (2) request, including commands; (3) question. It is not to be supposed that the very limited range and simple character of animal wants and ideas would necessarily bring into play the whole of this category of articulate speech. But, as a fact, they do need to use all three forms of expression, but omit the last. Unlike children, animals do not *ask* questions. They only 'look' them, and though they constantly and anxiously inquire what is to be done, how it is to be done, and the exact wishes of their masters, and occasionally even of other animals, the inquiry is made by the eye and attitude. A terrier, for instance, can almost transform his whole body into an animated note of interrogation.

Of the two remaining forms of speech—statement and request—the animals make very large use, but employ the latter in a far greater degree than the former. They use sounds for request, not only in particular cases in which they desire something to be done for them, but also in a great number of cases in which the request is a form of warning: 'Come!' 'Be careful!' 'Look out!' 'Go ahead!' 'Help!' The speech which indicates danger is sufficiently differentiated. Birds, for instance, have separate notes of warning to indicate whether the danger is in the form of a hawk or cat, or of a man. If a hawk, cat, or owl is on the move, the birds, especially blackbirds, always utter a clattering note, constantly repeated, and chickens have a special sound to indicate the presence of a hawk. But when disturbed by man the blackbirds have quite a different sound of alarm and the chickens also. Animals on the march are usually silent; but the hamadryad baboons use several words of command; and the cries of cranes and geese when flying in ordered flocks are very possibly signals or orders.

Specific requests are commonly made by a sound,

which the animal intends to be taken as expressing a want, while it indicates what it wants by showing the object. The greatest difficulty is when the object wanted, or required to be dealt with, is not present. The animal has then to induce you to follow and see the thing, and this often leads to great ingenuity both in the use of voice and action. This form of request is practised more or less successfully by a considerable number of the animals kept as pets or servants of man. Various monkeys, geese, a goat, a ewe with a lamb, elephants, cats very commonly, and dogs innumerable, are credited with 'accosting' persons, and bringing to their notice by vocal means the objects they desire or the actions they wish done. A most ingeniously constructed request of this kind was made a few years ago by a retriever dog late one night in London. The streets were empty; and the dog came up and, after wagging his tail, began to bark, using not the rowdy bark which dogs employ when jumping at a horse's head or when excited, but the persuasive and confidential kind of bark which is used in requests and reproaches. He was very insistent, especially when a small, dark passage was reached, up which he ran, still barking. As this did not answer, the dog ran back, took the writer's hand, in which he was carrying his glove, in his mouth, and gave a gentle pull in the direction of the passage. As this did not meet with the attention desired, the dog pulled the glove out of the hand and carried it off up the passage, keeping a few yards in front and waving its tail in a friendly way; this naturally led to pursuit, when the dog, still keeping ahead, dropped the glove in front of a gate leading into a butcher's yard, and began to bark again. As it obviously wanted the gate to be opened, this was done, and it trotted in without further remark. Everyone who has kept dogs knows the tone of the bark of request—a low 'wouf,' very unlike the staccato bark of anger, or vexation, or remonstrance. A bulldog at the Earl's Court Dog Show made his particular part of the bench almost unendurable by this form of bark, kept up (as we heard) for nearly three hours without a stop, because he was jealous of the attentions paid to the dog next him. This had won the first prize, and consequently received all the admiration; so the other dog barked short, sharp, incessant yelps at him all day long, only stopping when some one patted him. We believe that leopards are absolutely silent creatures; but many of the felidæ have a particular sound of request. In the cat a very short 'mew' is commonly used when the object is near, and will almost certainly be granted, such as the opening of the door, or the giving of water or milk. Unusual food which it fancies it will not get is asked for in another note; and any request not attended to is repeated in the different key. The tiger uses the low 'mew' in some form of conversation with the tigress; and the puma when domesticated has a considerable range of notes to ask for food, water, and society, or to return thanks; the latter being, as in the case of the cat and tiger, a kind of purr.

'Statement' in animal speech is mainly confined to indications that the creature has made a discovery, good or bad. For the former the cock has, perhaps, the most distinct set of sounds; they are quite unlike any other note he uses, and are confined to the assertion that he has found something good to eat. Cock pigeons do the same, and we imagine that geese have an equivalent sound. Dogs have two forms of sound to state a discovery, elephants only one. The dog barks loud and sharply over something new, or merely surprising. We have seen a dog barking in this way when a couple of geographical globes were placed in a window—objects he had never seen and wished to call attention to. But a painful discovery, such as that of a dead body, or a dangerously wounded man, is sometimes communicated by the dog howling, which marks a different form of speech. A practical acquaintance with shore shooting and the men who have learnt to imitate the notes of shore birds discloses some curious facts as to the minute differences between the 'talk' of different species. The greater number have a particular note which signifies 'Come'; and this note seems always to be understood and generally obeyed, almost instantly, by the birds of the same species, though no bird of another species pays the slightest attention to it. But the few shore birds which are really 'talkative'—namely, the wild geese, the redshank, and the green plover—pay very little attention to the calls either of their own species or of anyone who can imitate them. We never heard of anyone who has ever tried to 'call' wild geese. Green plover can be called, but very seldom; and though redshanks can sometimes be whistled within shot, this is rarely done.

The difference between the notes of invitation made by various shore fowl—stints, gray plover, golden plover, ringed plover, knots, and sandpipers—is so slight that no one but a fowler would notice it. Yet to these men the difference is as great as that between the sound of French and English. A really first-class gunner will sit in a creek in August and call the birds up, if within hearing and inclined to move, in any order you like to name. Even such closely allied birds as the curlew and the whimbrel have different notes, though, as they are so often associated on the marshes, one species will often answer to the call made by the other, probably in the expectation of finding some of its own tribe in the same place. It is not a little surprising that these different birds, most of which feed in company, should not have learnt a common 'all-fowls' tongue,' but they have not.* We once saw a large mixed flock of gray plover, knots, and stints flying past on the muds, at a distance of some ninety yards. A gunner noticed that there were two or three golden plover amongst them. These are easy to call; and all fowl are more likely to answer to the call when only two or three of the same species are together. The gunner, therefore, whistled the golden plovers' note, and out from the big flock of some sixty birds the pair of golden plovers instantly flew, wheeled round, and passed within fifty yards, answering the call in their own language. Perhaps the best instance of the dexterity of the gunners in learning bird-language was recently recorded in the *Westminster Gazette*. It is credited to a fowler who shot the only specimen of the broad-billed sandpiper ever killed in Norfolk. When down on the muds listening to the notes of the shore birds he distinguished one which he did not know. He imitated it, the bird answered, flew up to him, and was shot. It does not follow that talkative, garrulous species really have more to say to one another than others. Like other chatterboxes, they like to hear themselves, and do not listen to other people. Starlings, for instance, which seem almost to talk, and certainly

* In Mr. Tegetmeier's work on pheasants, it is noted that young golden pheasants bred under hens go gaping about for a day or two, as if stupid, before learning hens' language.

can imitate other birds when engaged in their curious
'song,' which seems so like a conversational variety
entertainment, are all the time enjoying a monologue.
No other starling listens. On the other hand, starlings,
when they have anything to say, as when nesting, or
quarrelling for places when going to roost, use quite
different notes. Of all bird-voices the song of the
swallow is most like human speech—not our speech,
but like the songs which the Lapps or such outlandish
races sing. A Lapp woman sings a song just like that
of a swallow at dawn. Yet the swallows seem really to
say little or nothing to one another, and never come to
each other's call. But the varieties of bird-speech, and
the possibilities of interchange of ideas, are very great.
If, for instance, there is any real foundation for the
stories of the rook-trials and stork-trials, speech must
play a considerable part in the proceedings.

XXXI.—ANIMALS UNDERGROUND

AN interesting find of buried treasure has recently been credited to a mole. Coins were seen shining in the earth of a freshly cast-up mole-hill at Penicuick, near Edinburgh, and a search showed that the mole had driven his gallery through a hoard of ancient coins of the date of Edward I.

Men of all countries seem agreed in regarding the work of animals underground as something quite normal and commonplace. Perhaps the best instance of this was the view long held by the Ostiaks of North Siberia that the mammoths whose bodies and bones they found embedded in the frozen soil were 'only' gigantic moles which worked deep down below ground, but were unlucky enough to come too near the top, and so were frozen! The facts are, however, in very strong contradiction to this view of the subterranean life of animals. Life underground and in the dark is absolutely contrary to the normal habits, tastes, and structure of almost all animals except the very few, like the common moles, tuco-tuco, and the marsupial sand-moles, which obtain their food below the earth-surface as diving birds catch fish below the sea-surface. It is almost an inversion of their normal way of life, and is probably due to some such compulsion as has also forced many animals to become nocturnal. Nor is it doubtful that if once this necessity were removed, their tendency would be to abandon this unnatural life, and return to the regions of light. How strong the pressure must have been which forced them underground may be gathered from the list of English terrestrial mammals. Twelve of these are bats; but of the remaining twenty-nine no less than sixteen, or more than half, live either wholly or partly underground. The list includes the fox, three shrews, the mole, the badger, the otter, three species of mice, two rats, three voles, and the rabbit. Besides there are several species of birds, as widely different in habit as the stormy petrel, sand-martin, puffin, sheldrake duck, and kingfisher, which for a time live in holes excavated in the earth. To abandon the sun, to bask in whose rays is to most animals one of the most agreeable of physical enjoyments, is an almost greater sacrifice than the relinquishment of fresh air. Yet the sacrifice is made, and the creatures, though not without occasional suffering and loss of health directly attributable to this cause, have succeeded in adapting themselves with great success to the new con-

LEAVING THE EARTH.

ditions. It might well be that the measure of this success decreased in proportion to the completeness with which the different species have adopted the underground habit and abandoned light and air. But in normal conditions this is not the case. The fox, whom we take to be the last of English mammals to become a burrower and dweller in holes—largely owing to the increase of fox-hunting and multiplication of packs of hounds—is an animal which spends as little time there as it can help, and has never ceased to suffer in health from the change. The earths become tainted, the foxes contract mange, and the spread of this fatal disease has increased yearly as the animals have become more subterranean, and, by taking their food into the earths, have converted them into larders as well as sleeping-places. How most of the burrowing animals find life endurable at all is difficult to discover. No one who has seen the colliers coming for their lamps and about to descend into the pit can have failed to note the marks of physical strain exhibited by all, from old men to boys. As each man or lad comes up and shouts the number of his lamp, the harsh, loud voices, the over-wrought lines of the face, and the general air of tension show that, however well satisfied the pitman is with his calling, *he* at least is not yet adapted to the underground life. But burrowing animals are among the merriest of the merry; there are few creatures more full of gaiety and buoyant spirits than a prairie-dog, or even a sandhill-rabbit; and we have only once seen an animal grimy from attempted burrowing, and that was an opossum which mistook a chimney for a hole in a hollow tree. Some have coats so close and fine that sand runs off them as water does from feathers; others have 'shivering muscles,' by which they can shake their jackets without taking them off. Rats, however, do object to some forms of dust, and will not burrow in it. An old Suffolk rat-catcher always laid ashes in the runs made by them beneath brick floors. His theory on the subject was that the ashes 'fared to make them snuffle.' But even if earth, dust, and clay do not adhere to the animals' coats when burrowing, the danger, or at least the discomfort, to the delicate surface of the eye would seem to afford an almost constant source of uneasiness to creatures burrowing in loose soil. And the eyes of most burrowing creatures are by no means protected against such damage. If the rat and the rabbit had a horn plate over their eyes, as a snake has, or overhanging eyebrows and deeply-sunk orbits, the modifications would be at once explained by evolution; but they exhibit no such modification whatever. On the contrary, both of them have prominent, rather staring eyes, without protection, and no eyelashes to speak of. We believe that, just as divers learn to keep their eyes open under water without feeling pain, so many of the mining animals can endure the presence of dust and grit on the eye without discomfort. Tame rats will allow dust or fine sand to rest on the eyeball without trying to remove it; and it may be inferred that rabbits, mice, voles and shrews can do the same. The mole's eyes have become so atrophied, that when a mole is skinned the eyes *come off with the skin;* but this is probably not because the mining hurts the eye, but because the mole, having learnt to work by scent and touch, had little further use for sight.

Ventilation, or rather the want of it, must be another difficulty in the underground life of almost all mammals. The rabbit and the rat secure a current of air by forming a bolt-hole in connection with their system of passages; but the fox, the badger, and many of the field voles and mice seem indifferent to any such precaution. There is no doubt that whatever gave the first impulse to burrow, many animals look upon this, to us, most unpleasant exertion as a form of actual amusement. It also confers a right of property. Prairie-dogs constantly set to work to dig holes merely for the love of the thing. If they cannot have a suitable place to exercise their talent in, they will gnaw into boxes or chests of drawers, and there burrow, to the great detriment of the clothes therein contained. In an enclosed prairie-dog 'town' they have been known to mine until the superincumbent earth collapsed and buried the greater number. A young prairie-dog let loose in a small gravel-floored house instantly dug a hole large enough to sit in, turned round in it, and bit the first person who attempted to touch him. Property gave him courage, for before he had been as meek as a mouse.

It is noticeable that the two weakest and least numerous of our mice, the dormouse and the harvest-mouse, do not burrow, but make nests ; and that these do not multiply or maintain their numbers like the burrowing mice and voles. But the fact that there are members of very closely allied species, some of which do burrow, while others do not, seems to indicate that the habit is an acquired one. In this connection it is worth noting that many animals which do not burrow at other times form burrows in which to conceal and protect their young, or, if they do burrow, make a different kind, of a more elaborate character. Among these nursery burrows are those of the dog, the fox, the sand-martin, the kingfisher, and the sheldrake. Foxhound litters never do so well as when the mother is allowed to make a burrow on the sunny side of a straw-stack. In time she will work this five feet or six feet into the stack, and keep the puppies at the far end, while she lies in the entrance. Vixens either dig or appropriate a clean burrow for their cubs, which is a

AN ANCIENT BRITON.

natural habit, or, at any rate, one acquired previously to the use of earths by adult foxes.

The sand-martins are, however, the most complete examples of creatures which have taken to underground life entirely to protect their young, and abandon it with joy the instant these have flown. How far the kingfisher and the sheldrake contribute to the making of the burrows in which they lay their eggs is doubtful, but it is a very notable change of habit in birds of such strong flight and open-air, active habits. It may be paralleled by the case of the stormy petrels and forktailed petrels, true ocean birds, which, nevertheless, abandon the sea and air to dig deep holes in the soil of the Hebridean islets, and rear their young in these dark and tortuous passages. Rabbits, rats, and some other rodents make nursery burrows of a very rudimentary kind, having only one opening, which the mothers close up when leaving the nest. This probably gives the clue to the process by which the true 'underground animals' have been evolved. First they scratched holes in which to shelter their young. Then they made use of the same device to protect themselves, and acquired much greater skill in working, and some modifications of coats and claws to do this with comfort and effect. In time the habit became so easy that its exercise afforded them pleasure; and thus we have the spectacle of the prairie-dog who digs holes for amusement. Another primitive instinct may also have contributed to develop the burrowing habit, namely, that of burying food. Dogs will scratch rudimentary burrows to do this, and there is no doubt that the rats, hamsters, field-voles, and other rodents felt the burrowing impulse in this connection. Some tame rats kept in a cage where they could not burrow were recently seen to cover their food up with small pebbles, which they fetched from the floor; but had it been possible to make a hole and so secrete it, they would no doubt have done so.

XXXII.—MAMMALS IN THE WATER

THE Zoo otters have conformed to the universal tendency to extend the range of diet by eating ship-biscuit as well as fish. They make believe that it is fish all the time, biting the biscuit into fragments, then pushing these into the water with their noses, chasing them and catching them, and, after the biscuit is well saturated, eating it on the bank. Incidentally, this shows how very prettily an otter eats its meals. It lies flat down, and holds the 'fish' neatly between its hands, 'thumbs upwards,' the hands being quite flat, like the two ends of a book-slide. The quickness and handiness of the otter in the water is most surprising, considering the very slight difference in general form between it and allied non-amphibious mammals ; there is practically nothing which a salmon or trout can do which the otter cannot beat, except the salmon's leap up a weir. It can even imitate that astonishing 'shoot' by which a trout goes off from its feeding-place like an arrow to the bank or weeds. It can also climb a pollard-tree, dig holes, dive in salt water, travel fast on land, and *run* at the bottom of the water.

Compared with the aquatic powers of civilized man —the only mammal, except a monkey, which does not swim naturally—these feats are very surprising; but the list of land animals which are expert swimmers is very much larger than might be supposed. It also embraces many classes of animals, and the number of the aquatic or semi-aquatic members of very different families suggests that the aquatic habit was at first only accidental, and that very many creatures which do not by habit swim and dive might, under other circumstances, have become aquatic. Judging from our own experience, one of the most difficult 'adaptations' of habit encountered in the amphibious life is that of keeping the eyes open under water, with no special protection. It is disagreeable in fresh and painful in salt water. Conceding that the really amphibious creatures have learnt to do this gradually—otters, water-voles, water-shrews, polar bears, and seals— how are we to account for the aquatic dexterity of a creature like the land-rat? A common brown rat can see under water as well as a water-rat can; it swims and dives equally well, and can burrow into a bank below the water. This is less creditable engineering than the sub-aquatic work of the beaver, which buries logs and fixes the foundations of the dam under

OTTER SWIMMING A STREAM.

water, but it shows that the rat is quite at home in that element. The rat has no structural adaptation of any kind to help him, and the water-vole is to all appearance the same in structure as the land-vole. That there should be so little modification is quite contrary to the ancient and established view that if an animal can swim and dive it *must* be like a duck or a fish. When Fuller was writing of the 'natural commodities' of Cardiganshire, he remarked: 'What plenty there was of beavers in this country in the days of Giraldus; the breed of them is now quite destroyed, and neither the fore-foot of a beaver (which is like a dog's) nor the hind-foot (which is like a goose's) can be seen therein.' But the performances of the creatures, which are little or not at all changed in structure, are perhaps more interesting from the personal point of view of their human critics than those of animals like the seals, walruses, and whales, whose legs have turned into fins. Their experiences and difficulties in the water *ought* to be somewhat like our own. The surprising point is that most forms of movement in the water seem to present to them no difficulty at all. Very young otters are 'taught' to go into the water, and so, presumably, are the young duckbills, which lie in a subterranean nest for several weeks before entering the water. But the young otters at the Zoo were hauled out by their mothers when they stayed in too long. They swam like young ducks, and the teaching was by example, not instruction. When master of the art, the otter swims, not with all four feet, but with the hind-feet, folding the front paws alongside its body. Mr. Trevor-Battye has noticed that the water-voles do the same. This agrees with the progress of human swimmers, who usually begin by making too much use of the arms and too little of the legs, but discover later on that the latter are the main aids in swimming either on or below the surface. The otters are so far modified from the polecat tribe that they have webbed toes; the water-voles have not even this advantage over their land relations. It ought to follow from this that the latter could, with a little trouble, become aquatic. There is a great deal of evidence to show that there is no hard-and-fast line between land mammals and water mammals, so far as this distinction rests on the *ability* to use both elements. Stoats, for instance, are excellent swimmers, and, if put to it for food, would probably learn to catch fish just as the polecat is known to catch eels. Cats, which have an intense dislike of wet, swim well, carrying the head high. Their distaste for aquatics does not extend to the larger cats. Tigers are fond of bathing, swim fast, and the 'river tigers' of the Sunderbunds, and the tigers near the coast of the Straits of Malacca, are constantly noticed in the water. Whether the trained Egyptian cats which were used to take waterfowl in the reed-beds by the Nile ever swam when stalking them does not appear from the ancient pictures ; but the extent to which the dog voluntarily becomes aquatic entitles some breeds to be considered amphibious. A dog belonging to a waterman living near one of the Thames ferries has been known to continue swimming out in the stream for an hour without coming to land. It did this for amusement on a fine Sunday morning. Another riverside dog was taught to dive, and fetch up stones thrown in which sank to the bottom. This dog would pick out stones from the bottom of a bucket of water, selecting one which it had been shown before from a number of others. It had so far become amphibious that it could use its eyes under water. In France otter-hound puppies are introduced to their aquatic life by setting their kettle of soup in a pond or stream, so that they must go in deep to feed. Soon they become as fast swimmers on the surface as the otter itself, though the physical advantages of submarine motion give the otter the advantage when it is below the surface.

As the land-rats and water-voles can swim and run below water, there is no reason to suppose that the various tribes of mice cannot do the same. The house-mouse swims on the surface as well as the rat, but it has, apparently, not yet learnt to dive. All the pachyderms can swim, and very many are as much at home in the water as on land. The story that pigs cut their own throats when swimming is a myth. To prove it, a whole family of pink pigs were chased into a fine muddy pond, and made to swim across. They swam well, and the 'contour line' of mud along their sides showed that their backs were above water as well as their heads. Elephants are almost as clever in the water as the polar bears. They can swim and *walk under* water without coming to the surface, keeping the trunk out of the water like a diver's tube. There is plenty of flexibility in an elephant's legs, enough, at all events, to use in swimming; but the properly aquatic hippopotamus can scarcely be said to swim—it rises and sinks at will, but it habitually walks or runs on the ground at the bottom of the river. Two South American river creatures seem unaccountably aquatic —the coypu, which might just as well be a land-rat, but is a water-rat in the process of becoming a beaver, and the capybara, which is a gigantic water guinea-pig. Each is quite at home in the rivers, and, as the capybara is aquatic, there seems no reason why the guinea-pigs or the Patagonian cavies should not learn to swim and dive, if circumstances made it useful. Even man himself becomes almost amphibious in certain regions. Temperature permitting, he swims as well and dives better than many of the animals mentioned above—better, for instance, than any dogs. The Greek sponge-fishers and the Arab divers must have sight almost as keen below water as that of the sea-otter. They have even learnt by practice to control the consumption of the air-supply in their lungs. The usual time for a hippopotamus to remain below water is five minutes. The pearl-fisher can remain below for two and a half minutes. In a tank a diver has remained under water four minutes. But *temperature* marks the limits of man's amphibious habits. Its effects seem less potent on other mammals in the water. The hairless amphibious beasts of the tropics — hippos, tapirs, elephants, and manatees—need warm waters to swim in; but in temperate Europe, or even in the Arctic seas, certain animals seem indifferent to constant wet, and the intense discomfort of 'wet clothes' when out of the water. A polar bear is wet, literally, to the skin. The otters, though they have an inner coat, look thoroughly drabbled when out of the water. The land-rat's coat also becomes wet through. The latter avoids water in cold weather; but the otters sit cheerfully on the bank in winter frosts or even in wind. So do the Zoo beavers, but their lower fur is probably impervious to wet. A piece of beaver fur, with the long coat taken off, was dry at the roots after soaking for two and a half hours in a basin. If the temperature of aquatic animals were naturally low, like that of a fish, their indifference might be explained. A hibernating dormouse is as cold as death ; a tame rat, tested by a clinical thermometer, showed a temperature of one hundred degrees, and a live otter can scarcely be of lower temperature than a live cat or a Cape ratel. The Zoo caution, 'These animals bite,' precludes any effort at taking their normal heat ; but that of a rat, which takes to the water freely when the March winds are blowing, is normal, and there is no reason to suppose that that of the otter is different.

As chill to the surface tissues is always dangerous to warm-blooded creatures, in the absence of an inner layer of fat which the whale, and, in some degree, the polar bear, possesses, the fur must be the non-conductor which protects them. Water, unless in movement, is not a quick conductor of heat. The fur, aided by the outer and longer hairs which keep it in place, holds the water-jacket motionless, even if it reaches to the skin, and this 'water compress' saves the animal from a chill. If the cold winds extract the warmth from it when standing wet through on land, it takes to the water as the relatively warmer element.

XXXIII.—CROCODILES

Mr. E. Stewart, in a paper in the *Contemporary Review* on crocodile-shooting, contributes much interesting information as to the numbers and habits of these creatures in India. The largest and most dangerous to human life of the Indian species is the salt-water crocodile of the estuaries (*C. porosus*). This sometimes reaches thirty feet in length, and cruises for its prey like a shark, occasionally swimming some distance out to sea. But the creature with which Mr. Stewart is mainly concerned is the marsh crocodile, the 'mugger' of the inland rivers. Its numbers are very great, and do not diminish. On one small river, the Tiljooga in Tirhoot, a stream not more than ten or twelve yards broad, but very deep, crocodiles might be seen every sixty yards, singly or in groups, which took toll of men, dogs, and cattle, as well as fish. What a curse they are to the inhabitants of the riverine districts may be gathered from the fact that the village watering-places have to be palisaded to keep these creatures out, and that in spite of this a big 'bull crocodile' will attach himself permanently to some such spot, just as a pike frequents a particular pool, and live on the toll he takes from the village. He is then known as a '*burka luggaree goh*,' or 'crocodile moored like a boat.'

Such a beast is the subject of Mr. Rudyard Kipling's story, 'The Undertaker,' in which the 'mugger of Mugger Ghaut' tells his own tale. His feasts of drowned carrion, his constancy to the ford and the bathing 'ghaut,' where he carries off men, women, and children, and his adventures when he changes his quarters to distant haunts by using small tributaries, creeks, and irrigation cuts, are all strictly in keeping with the observations of Mr. Stewart and other Indian naturalists. The former adds some ghastly corroboration to the details of this autobiography of a 'mugger,' though, incidentally, he mentions that this name is English, not Indian. When out tiger-shooting he came across a huge crocodile sleeping on the bank of a small stream—for crocodiles will travel up the smallest waterways at certain seasons, and populate any pools formerly free from them. The crocodile was shot, and his men at once cut it open to extract the gall-bladder, which is looked upon as a valuable charm. Inside this creature's stomach were two skulls and the putrid remains of as many bodies. He also witnessed a crocodile's attack on children at a bathing-ghaut. The creature was swimming on the surface, holding a little native girl in its mouth, while the father was paddling in pursuit in a canoe, and striking the creature with a bamboo. It dropped its victim, but she was so frightfully injured that she died. Mr. Kipling notes that the 'parish' mugger, which had taken toll of the inhabitants of the village since it was founded, was in time raised to the dignity of a 'godling,' or local fetich. This seems to show the process by which the crocodile-worship became gradually stereotyped in parts of ancient Egypt, the creature being propitiated *because* it was a pest. Herodotus is careful to mention that it was only in some villages that the creature was worshipped. His words are: 'Among some of the Egyptians the crocodile is sacred, while others pursue him as an enemy. The inhabitants of Thebais and of the shores of Lake Mœris regard him with veneration. Each person has a tame crocodile. He puts pendants of glass and gold in its ear-flaps, and gives it a regular allowance of food daily. When it dies it is embalmed. . . . But the inhabitants of Elephantine eat the crocodile, and do not think it sacred at all.' Possibly these were the villages which suffered most from ' parish crocodiles,' while others which were not so cursed, or had a more enterprising population, cheerfully angled for them, and probably, as they do now, cooked and ate them. At Dongola they were formerly rather proud of their crocodile stews, and the flavour of the animal was considered to be superior there to that of 'down-river crocodiles,' just as some people praise an Arundel sole or an Amberley trout.

Herodotus, to whose method of setting down what he saw or heard, however incredible it might appear, time is always doing justice, has two excellent testimonials as to his crocodile stories. One is Strabo, and the other Mr. Brehm. Strabo was taken by a priest to see a sacred crocodile kept in a pond at Arsinoe. 'Our host,' he writes, 'who was a person of importance, and our guide to all sacred sights, went with us to the tank, taking with him from a table a small cake, some roast meat, and a small cup of mulled wine. We found the crocodile lying on the bank. The priests immediately went up to him, and while some of them opened his mouth, another put in the cake and crammed down the meat, and finished by pouring in the wine.' We are not surprised to hear that after the last dose the crocodile 'jumped into the water and swam away.' Brehm saw what Herodotus did not see, the manners and customs of the crocodiles on the White Nile at the time when the river-bed becomes the resort of the greater part of the bird population of that portion of the Soudan. This occurs at low Nile, when the water-supply elsewhere disappears, and the sandbanks are the nightly resting-place of millions of cranes, storks, ibises, pelicans and geese. In the evening these sandbanks are white, gray, or crimson, from the solid masses of birds, the most brilliant of which are the tantalus ibises. By night these feathered crowds are constantly 'rushed' by the crocodiles, which during this season live more on fowls than on fish. The incredible number of the birds is maintained from two sources: part are recruited by the migrants from Europe and Asia; part are native birds which have reared their young earlier, and bring them to the river when the African Steppe is too parched to yield food. Among these native birds is the 'zic-zac,' which Herodotus called the trochilus. Now, as then, it is the constant attendant of the crocodile, and spends its whole life on the sandbanks, which these monsters also haunt. Brehm not only watched it feeding round the crocodiles, and even prying into their open jaws—as these creatures commonly sleep with their mouth open and the lower jaw dropped —but also noted their extreme cunning in other respects. At the season of low Nile the crocodile bird is more constant to the sandbanks even than the crocodiles themselves. The latter only use them to bask on by day; the birds sleep there and lay their eggs on the sand. Brehm, though certain that they were nesting, could not succeed in finding their eggs. One day he saw a bird give two or three scratches with its feet before it flew off the bank. He swept away the sand and found that underneath it were the eggs. The crocodile bird, like the crocodile, buries its eggs, though it takes the trouble to hatch them itself.

Crocodiles are now credited with one virtue—the only one ever ascribed to them. Some species make a nest, and others are very jealous and bold in defending their eggs. The nest-making crocodile is the estuary species (*C. porosus*), 'the man-eating crocodile *par excellence* of the East,' according to Mr. H. P. Carter. It makes a mound of river vegetation, and leaves this to hatch the eggs when the mass ferments, on the plan adopted by the mound-making birds of Australia. Near this nest it keeps watch, much after the manner of a cock swan. It is on record that this is one of the very few nests which the native boy respects, without any deterrent local opinion. But the 'mugger' is also a careful parent while its eggs are hatching. Mr. Stewart notes that the female 'mugger' always watches by its eggs, and drives off not only human beings, but dogs and crows that approach the place where they are hidden in the sand. The discovery that 'crocodile skin' makes the most beautiful *natural* leather in the world was due to accident. Sportsmen who had killed specimens and wished to bring home the horn-plated hides as trophies, had the whole skin tanned. This included not only the plated portion, but the sides, neck and belly of the creature. The handsome markings and 'grain' of the skin, and the fine tone taken by the leather, were remarked. Before long bags of crocodile-hide were made in New York for visitors who had brought the leather from Florida. It then became fashionable for the most luxurious form of bag, dressing-case, and leather trinkets; and though it is less durable than pigskin, being liable to split where the deeper markings cross, it remains the most popular material for this kind of *article de luxe*. Most of this leather is alligator skin, not crocodile, and the main supply comes from the swamps and rivers of Florida. In this exquisite climate, and among the quays, streams, coral reefs and lakes of the peninsula, the life of birds and fish seems almost at its maximum intensity. But wonderful as are the swarms of sea-birds—pelicans, cormorants and herons—the fish population is even more extraordinary, because not only the numbers, but the size of the species is incredibly augmented by the vast supply of food. There the herring is represented by the gigantic tarpon, five feet long; and sharks, monstrous barracoutas, giant turtles and other maritime monsters swarm in the warm rivers and salt lagoons. There the alligators, fed on this bountiful fare, swarm also; and great as is the demand for their skins, alligator-shooting by night still yields a plentiful supply, and affords a novel, if rather tame, sport. Each shooter fastens a dark lantern to his cap, and thus equipped sits in the bows of a canoe, and like some luciferous monster of the deep seas, shoots the beams ahead across the swamps. Soon he sees round the fringe of the lake numbers of pairs of twinkling lights—alligators' eyes reflecting the beams of his lantern. Mr. A. C. Harmsworth, who describes this sport in 'The Encyclopædia of Sport,' dwells with much enthusiasm on these scenes by night on the Florida lakes. The largest alligators are known by the width between the shining orbs, which are all that is visible of their bodies. When shot, they are at once gaffed, and the skins are kept by the shooters and sent to be tanned for further use. They are then a far more durable and more useful trophy than most skins and hides of big game, for there are few rooms in which chairs and other furniture covered with soft-tanned crocodile skin are not ornamental. On the Nile crocodiles are not found below the second cataract; but Sir Samuel Baker constantly lost men, when in command of the Khedival troops on their way to Gondokoro, from the attacks of these creatures. They not only dragged their victims from the sterns of the boats, but came up into the shallows in the evening, like pike, and caught his soldiers when bathing and fetching water, even in the docks where his steamers lay. Neither on the Nile nor in India has the trade in 'crocodile skin' become a popular industry. When the supply fails in Florida, we may hope that these pests of tropical rivers will be thinned off. They have survived too long already.

XXXIV.—MARSUPIALS AND THEIR SKINS

PRESENT prices will certainly not alter the English feeling that the wearing of fur is a luxury, and a most expensive one. A series of very severe winters might force us to change this view, because it would become evident that to preserve health fur must be worn by men as well as by women, and we should discover, as everyone in Northern Europe discovered long ago, that the greater number of furs are not dear, but cheap, and that these cheap furs come into the market by millions at a time. This applies to the skins of the musquash, gray squirrel, and hamster, besides which the sheepskins and lambskins which our nation never has worn, and probably never will consent to wear, except in the far less warm manufactured form, number as many millions more. But far the greatest number of fur-bearing animals killed, though their skins are not all brought to market, are the marsupials—the opossums, wombats, kangaroos, and wallabies (smaller kangaroos) of the Australian continent. This ought to be the great reserve of good and cheap fur. Yet it is among these creatures that the greatest waste of fur-bearing animals occurs.

Opossum-skin rugs are familiar objects in this country, but the skins of the larger marsupials are rarely seen or used. Yet in many parts of Australia they are now exterminated, partly that their hides may be used for leather, partly to preserve the grass they eat as food for sheep. It is said that ninepence per scalp was paid by Government for each one shot. The large kangaroos and many kinds of wallaby have a coat so close and soft that it will lie in any direction, like plush. It consists almost entirely of 'under-fur,' and the natural tints are very beautiful—some French gray, others warm red, with tints of orange and rose colour, others like rough beaver or nutria skin. The common 'opossum' of Australia has a far less compact, though deeper fur, which often comes off when much worn; and though the dark Tasmanian variety has a splendid tint, its looseness and depth cause it to harbour dust, and make it difficult to clean. Nevertheless, the yearly 'catch' of opossums beats that of any other fur animal. It is conducted without sense or moderation; for the creatures are constantly killed in the summer, and the skins, then almost worthless, are shipped to England. The wombats, or 'native bears,' are also killed off for the sake of their fur, which is used in considerable quantities in this country for making hearthrugs.

But the whole race and nation of kangaroos, wallaroos, and wallabies are being destroyed without any use being made of their fur at all. In Australia a wallaby rug, almost as fine as beaver skin, can be bought for two pounds. In England we make them into shoe-leather. The demand for this alone threatens to exterminate most of the species, just as in time the new material, 'electric sealskin'—made from rabbit-fur —may kill off the plague of Australian rabbits. But in that case we shall have the fur in the form of 'electric seal' as a memorial. The growing scarcity of the 'great original' of all kangaroos was shown in a practical manner three years ago, when the 'boxing kangaroo' was in the height of his fame. This animal was said to have earned twenty thousand pounds in twelve months; and whether this sum was correctly stated or not, it was admitted at the Royal Aquarium that he had made more money than any other animal —more, even, than the most celebrated racehorses had earned, whether in training or after. Now, though this particular 'old man' kangaroo boxed every day with a regularity and apparent zeal which would not have discredited a human professional, the secret of this performance lay not in any special teaching of the animal, but in the cleverness by which his owner had noted that a tame kangaroo, when not afraid of his owner, always 'boxes' if he is sparred with, putting up his short fore-arms and paws directly the man's hands approach his nose, and retaliating by blows like those which a rabbit gives with its fore-feet. One of the wallabies at the Zoo does exactly the same, and even punches its keeper in the back if after a round or two he turns to leave the cage. A small fortune was waiting for anyone who could get a good large 'boomer' kangaroo, reasonably tame, in time to set him boxing before the novelty wore out. But though the great gray kangaroo was quite cheap and common in menageries twenty years ago, it was discovered that the visible supply in Europe had dwindled almost to nothing. The dealers could count the available specimens on the fingers of one hand, and as these were in the gardens of learned societies, they were not for sale. The price rose from the nominal one of twelve pounds to sixty pounds. The Dublin Zoo were offered eighty pounds for one which they had bought for forty pounds, and refused the double price. The few specimens in the Continental zoological gardens were bought early by speculative showmen, and resold at huge profits; and a syndicate which was formed later to exhibit a boxing kangaroo in Paris at an engagement of three hundred pounds a week had to be broken up because not one could be obtained. Every kangaroo in Europe outside the Zoological Gardens was boxing nightly. By the time some fresh specimens had been obtained in Australia and shipped to England the excitement had subsided. But the female 'boomer' still costs from forty to fifty pounds—rather a high price for a creature which was recently being killed off as a troublesome species of vermin.

Our climate suits both the great gray kangaroo and the much scarcer great red kangaroo, and these, with many of the smaller species, are bred in the Zoological Gardens, and are readily acclimatized. The kangaroos, large and small, have something of the adaptability of rabbits, and are at home in most conditions of soil and weather. They are found from the burning plains to the tops of the rocky ranges of the interior, and from the snowy tops of Mount Wellington, in Tasmania, to the forests in the lowest valleys. Damp does not seem to hurt them, yet they will bask for hours in the hottest sun, lying exposed upon the rocks. As early as 1863 John Gould gave it as his opinion that they would 'doubtless readily become acclimatized in this country.' Recently many large proprietors have taken a fancy to them, and stocked their parks. Sir E. G. Loder has introduced the great kangaroo and two species of wallaby into his park at Horsham; Mr. Naylor Leyland has a number at Haggerston Castle, in Northumberland; and those kept by Lord Rothschild at

Tring have become common objects of the district. At large, when feeding or lying on their sides in all kinds of graceful poses, with their 'hands' drooping languidly, and their large watchful eyes turned in the direction of their visitor, they are almost as pretty as deer, and the beauty of their fur is far greater than that of most of the *cervidæ*. This may be seen even at the Zoo, where they are kept in very small runs, which give them no adequate room for exercise, and hinder the proper development of their fur. In the great red kangaroo, the fur of the male (born in the Gardens) is deep, soft, and woolly, a mixture of brick-red and gray. On the throat the colour heightens to a warm rose colour. The fur of the female is a beautiful French gray, and both tints and texture are admirable in both. Of the many species of kangaroo and wallaby living outside the tropical belt of Australia, there are few which, if killed at the proper season, would not supply a handsome, warm, and durable lining-fur for coats at a low price. Here, however, kangaroo skins are used solely for leather, japanned boots being largely made from them, and the fur is scraped off and mixed with other 'oddments' which form material for felt. Six thousand five hundred *bales* of kangaroo skins were recently bought for this purpose at a single sale, and with them those of eighty-five thousand wallabies and fifty-five thousand wombats, or 'native bears.' At another sale over one hundred thousand wallaby skins and seventy-three thousand wombat skins were offered, the former being only half the number accumulated for the corresponding half of the year before.

To point out that the marsupials ought to have a value as fur-bearing animals may not lead to any less wholesale destruction than goes on at present. There is no surer way to diminish the quantity of any natural product than to create a demand for it in Europe.* In the early days they were killed by the squatters and not even skinned. The carcases were left to rot. Later, they have been slaughtered partly as vermin, partly for the sake of the leather. In the future, it may be hoped that if it be necessary to kill them, they will be hunted when the fur is in condition, and that the stock of handsome, warm, and inexpensive fur of the larger marsupials will find a place among the regular winter clothing of English wearers.

* Two thousand kangaroo tails were received in condition to make soup of by a London firm in the summer of 1898, and sold so well that a fresh consignment was ordered.

XXXV.—WILD BEASTS' SKINS IN COMMERCE

THE last few years have seen a marked disappearance from the leather industry of a form of supply which should never have reached the dimensions it attained—the hides of countless wild beasts. No one grudges to the purposes of trade the hides of the alligator or the shark, still less those of domesticated animals or of big game killed for food. But for more than twenty years there have come to the markets of America and Europe hundreds of thousands of hides, destined for the commonest commercial uses, stripped from wild animals which have been killed for the value of the hide alone. Whole species have been butchered to the last individual to make shoe-leather. To say which country has been the greatest offender would be difficult. There is not much room for distinction between the 'skin-hunters' of North America, South Africa, or Australia. But in the former country at least, the State Governments are adopting vigorous measures to stop this repulsive industry, and by limiting the number of deer which may be killed by individuals, prevent such destructive waste of animal life. We wish that these laws could be extended to all British Colonies and dependencies. Wherever big game has entirely disappeared from districts where it formerly abounded, and wherever whole species have been exterminated, the mischief has in nearly every case been done not to procure food, but solely to obtain the creatures' skins. It is not the big-game hunter, or the savage, or even the agriculturist, who destroys the creatures, but the 'skin-hunter.' In every 'new country' this wasteful and relentless enemy of animal life has always appeared with the regularity of some recurring plague, and made it his business to destroy every creature larger than a hare.

The advent of the skin-hunter takes places at a particular period of development in recent settlements. He is never among the early pioneers, but is a kind of parasite in half-occupied territories, often intensely disliked by the resident squatters, as he destroys the game on which they partly depend, though he sometimes succeeds in converting these to his own evil ways. In South Africa, for instance, the early Boer settlers, like the early pioneers of North America, killed the antelopes for meat, and used their skins for clothing. They ate the venison, and from the hides they made suits of leather—'shamoyed,' not tanned—supple, soft, and comfortable garments, well suited for the life on the veldt. The number of animals killed was limited by their own personal needs and those of their families. About 1850 the Boers learnt that the myriads of antelope, quagga and zebra which wandered over the plains had a marketable value other than as food or supplying leather hunting-shirts. The skin-hunters taught them that though the bodies of the creatures might be left to rot on the veldt, the hides, not tanned or dressed, but merely stripped from the body, were marketable, to supply the European demand for leather. The country was just sufficiently opened up to have arrived at the stage at which the business of the skin-hunter pays. Freight is high, but not too high, and though hides of countless cattle and sheep may be had for little enough in the settled districts, the skins of the wild animals cost nothing at all, except the value of powder and shot. Even this was economized in South Africa. 'The Boers of the pastoral Republic became perfect adepts at skin-hunting,' writes Mr. Bryden. 'They put in just sufficient powder to drive the missile home, and carefully cut out their bullets for use on future occasions. So lately as 1876, when I first wandered in Cape Colony, I well remember the waggons coming down from the Free State and Transvaal, loaded up with nothing but the skins of blesbok, wildebeest, and springbok. This miserable system of skin-hunting has been, and still is where any game remains, pursued in all native States of South Africa. Between 1850 and 1875 it is certain that some millions of these animals must have been destroyed in the Transvaal and Orange Free State.' The slaughter was so prodigious, and the variety of wild animals so great, in these wild regions of South Africa, that the result made a sensible difference in the leather industry of Europe. The markets were filled with skins which, when tanned, gave leather of a quality and excellence never known before, but the origin of which, as the material was still sold under old names, purchasers never suspected. Hides of the zebra and quagga arrived in tens of thousands; and good as horse-hide is for the uppers of first-class boots, these were even better. Smart Englishmen for years wore boots the uppers of which were made of zebra and quagga skin, or from the hides of elands, oryx, and gemsbok disguised under the names of 'calf' or patent leathers.

These South African game skins became a commercial article, relied upon for many years as part of the regular supply. It is amusing to note that quagga-skins are still quoted as part of this, the fact being that the last of the quaggas was killed years ago to fill the skin-hunter's pocket. In Mashonaland and

Central Africa the trade still flourishes, though only the poorest of the Boers follow it, and they have to trek north of the Limpopo. The hides of the larger bucks, such as the sable antelope, the roan antelope, the hartebeest, or of any of the zebras, are worth eight shillings or nine shillings each, and there is now something to be made by selling heads and horns as curiosities. Leather made from the skins of these big antelopes is still in common use in high-class boot-making. No one knows exactly what animal may not have supplied the uppers or soles of his foot-gear, and the possibilities range from the porpoise and the Arctic hair-seal, to the blesbok or the koodoo. Three other African animals' skins are in commercial demand for curiously different purposes. The giraffes, as everyone knows, are killed so that their skins may be made into sandals for natives and sjambok whips for colonists. In the Soudan they are also killed for the sake of their hides, which are made into shields. Many of the Dervish shields captured during their attempt to invade Egypt under the Emir Njumi were made of this material. The elephant and rhinoceros skins go to Sheffield. There they are used to face the wheels used in polishing steel cutlery. No other material is equally satisfactory, and it would be most difficult to find a substitute. The rhinoceros-skin used was formerly that of the white rhinoceros. Now that this species is extinct, the black rhinoceros of Central Africa is killed for the purpose. Much of this immensely thick skin, which is not tanned, but used in the raw state, never leaves Africa. It is in great demand for making the round shields used by the Arabs and Abyssinians. A black rhinoceros's hide yields eight large squares, each of which will make a round shield two feet in diameter, and each of these squares, even in the Soudan, is worth two dollars. The skin when scraped and polished is semi-transparent, like hard gelatine, and takes a high polish. Giraffe-skin is even more valued as material for shields, as it is equally hard and lighter. Thus, while the South African giraffes are killed off to supply whips, those of North Central Africa are hunted to provide the Mahdi's Arabs with shields.

In North America skin-hunting is a business entirely apart from that of the trapper, who only seeks furs. It destroyed the bison, and would now exterminate the deer, were it not that the Government has checked the trade by stringent laws enforcing a close time. It was for their hides or 'robes' that the buffalo herds were destroyed—not for their meat. This was perhaps the most notable achievement in all the history of this wasteful and selfish trade. In 1869 the Union Pacific Railway was completed, and divided the bison into two great hordes. Between 1872 and 1874 the southern horde was practically exterminated by the skin-hunters.

In summer the hides were stripped for leather, while those taken in winter were sold to be dressed for buffalo robes. The leather was no better than that of ordinary cattle. The 'robes' had a considerable value as winter wraps. The deer were less easily killed off, but for years an enormous trade was done in American deer-skins. These were mainly those of the black-tailed deer. The skin-hunter on his trained pony went out into the spruce-forests of the Rocky Mountains, killed his five or six deer every day, skinned them, and leaving the carcases to rot, took the hides back to his camp. When one district was 'shot out' he moved on to another, and having secured as many skins as his pack-horses could carry, took them to the nearest point on the railway, and sent them to New York. Side by side with the illicit skin-hunting, and its resultant trade in skins for tanning, there is a genuine demand in Canada for deer-skins for garments. Its main use is for leggings and moccasins to be worn with snow-shoes, or without snow-shoes, in winter. These moccasins are sold in great numbers, and nothing quite so comfortable has yet been devised as foot-gear in the dry Canadian snows. Their softness prevents the straps of the snow-shoes from galling the feet, and the leather is both porous and warm. It is not tanned but 'shamoyed,' the process which all races, civilized or savage, use when preparing wild beasts' skins for use as clothes other than boots. But the finest of all these soft leathers are the deer-skins used for gloves. Nothing is quite equal to this material for the purpose, and when genuine, it is the most expensive of any. Reindeer skin, fallow deer skin, and that of the fawns of many of the American species are used. 'Elk' gloves are not deer-skin at all, but an imitation. Much of the deer-skin is made into 'white leather,' in the same way that parchment, sheep-skin, and vellum are prepared for special purposes. The white buck-skin is used for leather breeches and military gloves, all military tailoring being of the most expensive material. Camel-skin, which used to be the favourite material for covering the trunks used in Indian travel sixty years ago, is now never employed for this purpose. Block-tin boxes are found more durable for all climates, but the old trunks may still be seen in Anglo-Indian houses, and the skin is often sound, though the wooden frame has decayed. The skins of large snakes are imported for making trinkets, while those of sharks are valuable to cover the 'grips' of sword-hilts. Even the cobra's skin is an article of commerce, being used by the Chinese to cover their one-stringed fiddles.

XXXVI.—EAGLES ON AN ENGLISH LAKE

Not the least interesting result of the last century of man's relations with wild animals in England is the survival of the large raptorial birds, and of a great proportion of our English mammals.

The attraction which preserved areas of water have not only for wild fowl, but for much rarer and larger birds, is scarcely realized by most proprietors. Yet there are some lake sanctuaries, even in England south of the Trent, which tempt not only the passing osprey, but such birds as the sea eagle and the peregrine falcon, to linger, the former for many months, and the latter often throughout the year, by their well-stocked waters. It is precisely those lakes which are kept most quiet and are least often seen by the public which are thus honoured by these interesting and exclusive visitors. Nor is it necessary to state here the exact site of these sanctuaries. But the following facts may be of interest to those who desire to see the stock of indigenous birds increased by others of marked beauty and interest.

One famous lake near our East Coast has been haunted by sea eagles since the year 1860. During the last twenty-five years it is believed that the eagles have paid more than fourteen visits to these waters, and remained not for a day or two, but for weeks and months. Their appearance is so well known in that neighbourhood that it has become part of the folk-lore of the district. Contrary to ancient belief, the eagles' visits are held to be unlucky, and facts are quoted to prove it. Omens from birds are proverbially ambiguous and uncertain, but the existence of this belief is itself evidence of the frequency and permanence of these eagle visits. On one occasion two eagles remained from the autumn to the early months of the following spring. They were frequently seen soaring high over the mansion, and it was noticed that one was smaller than the other. Generally the eagles come singly. The time of their arrival is usually in October, and their stay is commonly protracted until after Christmas. The birds are always of the white-tailed species, not golden eagles. But as the former are quite as large as the latter, the source from which such a voracious and formidable creature finds a living easily enough to keep it for months near an English country house is not at first obvious. The character of the lake explains this in part. It is situated in a very large park of more than three thousand acres, some of which is cultivated, enclosed by a wall nine miles round. The lake is at the edge of this park, about a mile from the sea; but the intervening marshes are strictly preserved, and the owner never allows the eagles to be shot, in spite of their raids on his game and wild-fowl. The park and the lake itself supply the sea eagles with game in such abundance that they are not tempted to roam.

The main food-supply of the birds is derived from the hares which swarm in this enclosed park. The area is large enough for a good estate in itself, and is heavily stocked with all kinds of game. It is said to be quite dangerous to ride a bicycle by night through the park, as the hares *will* hop up when they see the light, and sit on the roads, and have caused more than one bad spill by being run over. At daybreak the eagle leaves the tree in which he roosts near the lake, and rushes down on some unlucky hare. One was disturbed just after he had caught his hare. It was already dead, with its eyes picked out. The eagles usually eat the head first, then the body, bones and all, and leave nothing but the skin. They do attack other game, as one was seen in full chase after a partridge. But the hares form the mainstay of their food-supply. This is supplemented by two contributions from the lake itself. For many years this piece of water has been kept as a sanctuary, though shooting on a large scale goes on in the adjacent covers in the park. From

October until March it swarms with wild ducks. Sometimes not less than two thousand ducks and widgeon, with other species, are on the water. There is also a heronry, and a large flock of half-wild Canada geese. Gulls also come here in numbers, while coots and waterhens abound. This writer has not met among the many persons who have watched the eagles one who has seen an eagle kill a wild duck, though they often 'harry' the flocks, and create the most dismal terror amongst them. But the remains of duck are often found which are believed to have been killed by the eagles, and with these the bodies of gulls. It is, however, very possible that these birds are killed by the peregrine falcons, of which we say something later. Neither do they attack the Canada geese, though these large and conspicuous birds are constantly in flight between the lake and some adjacent marshes, and must offer a good mark for the eagle's swoop. But the lake, besides wild fowl, holds a great quantity of fish, among them numbers of big bream, running to 6 lb. or 7 lb. in weight. These big bream are liable to sickness in the spring, when the waters 'break,' and are full of weed, and float up to the top of the water lying on their sides. They then form a favourite dish for the sea eagles, which flap over the waters, and, dropping their feet, pick up the fish and devour them on the bank. The flight of the eagles is peculiar. As they hang round the lake all day, and do not travel any distance from the waters, they spend most of their time sitting in some big tree near the margin. When they take a flight, they look like enormous owls flapping across the park on some misty December day. If one flies down the centre of the lake, the ducks either rise in a body and fly out to sea, or take a short flight, and then, as the eagle overhauls them, drop like stones on to the surface. One of the most instantaneous panics among the ducks caused by an eagle was one bright winter day, when the surface was all frozen, except some two acres at the lower end, where about a thousand ducks were collected. Suddenly the whole mass of ducks rose and flew, with a noise like an explosion. The disturber was an eagle, which flew suddenly round a wood and over the lake.

Peregrine falcons seem never absent from this lake, and *they* kill and eat the wild ducks, teal, and widgeon, which are possibly too quick for the eagles. Recently, in April, the writer was watching a bunch of widgeon, with a few teal, flying up the lake, when a peregrine dashed after them, overtook them in a second, caught a teal, and carried it for some twelve yards, and then dropped it. The teal twisted round, flew back in the opposite direction, and then dropped on the water, evidently unhurt. This was only the falcon's 'fun,' for they never *kill* a bird over the water, though when a duck is flying over the park it is cut over and devoured. The sight was most curious, for the teal's head was bent down, while that of the falcon was thrown back; the falcon's tail was also bent downwards so as to be nearly vertical; it carried the teal in front of its body, not underneath it. 'Bustling the ducks' is a regular game with the peregrines, which feed early in the morning, and amuse themselves with tormenting the ducks in the afternoon. One will chase a flock of mallards up the lake, then another dashes out to meet them, and enjoys the sport of seeing the whole flock drop from air to water. This is a very exceptional sanctuary, but there are very many lakes where the same degree of protection might be rewarded by a similar confidence on the part of the birds; and though the eagles and falcons frighten the ducks, they do not drive them permanently from the waters. In Norfolk the white-tailed eagles were formerly common visitors to the Broad district, where they were known as 'fen eagles'; probably they were young birds passing south; but if these birds were less persecuted by the Scotch shepherds, their fidelity to this English lake shows that they might reappear on other waters of the East and South. Unfortunately, while the golden eagles are increasing in the deer forests, the sea eagles, which keep to the coast, and nest mainly near the sheep-farms, are persecuted and killed off as much as possible by the shepherds. Even poison is used against them, as they cause some loss among the young lambs. Doubtless the loss is not exaggerated. But while wealthy and public-spirited landowners extend a welcome to the birds in England, Highland lairds might do something to preserve them in their breeding-places.

XXXVII.—THE GREAT FOREST EAGLE

WITH the survival of the white-tailed eagle in our own over-populated islands, we may contrast the discovery two years ago of the largest eagle in the world in an island which has almost no inhabitants at all. Mr. John Whitehead, a naturalist who has devoted much time to the exploration of the different islands of the Philippine group, formed, among other collections of birds made in this region, a series of those inhabiting the island of Samar. This collection was lost at sea near Singapore, and in order to replace it and restore the lost link in his chain of examples of 'island life' in this little-known region, he once more set out from Manilla in 1896 and established himself again in the woods of Samar. In doing so he had no other choice than to become one of the inhabitants of the tropical forest. Samar is all forest, and there was no more escape from it than there is from the desert or the steppe for those who elect to travel in Arabia or Central Asia. The great tropical forest which belts the world is very much the same, whether in Central America, or the Amazons, or the islands of the Malay Archipelago. Its peculiarity from the human point of view is that life goes on on two levels. There is an upper story and a basement. The basement is the ground, on which by the strict law of the forest no creature is supposed to live at all, except perhaps the few species of forest swine which, with various differences of form, haunt the great forests in America and the Malay Archipelago. But of all ground-dwelling creatures which venture into this 'crypt' of the tropical forest, man is at the greatest disadvantage. He walks beneath a roof of foliage so lofty that he can scarcely distinguish the forms of the branches which support its leaves, supposing that there were light sufficient to use his sight to good purpose. But the tops of the giant trees are so dense that light scarcely penetrates, and the would-be explorer of the forest, and discoverer of new species of birds and beasts, finds that he has to tread the mazes of a temple of twilight, in which all the life, light, and beauty exist, not below and within, but upon the roof. On the side remote from earth life goes on gaily, and with such completeness, that not only do the birds, insects, and monkeys enjoy a world of their own, but in the cups and reservoirs of the gigantic flowers and creepers water-insects and molluscs live and reproduce themselves without ever coming in contact with the ground.

In the island of Samar this impracticable forest is found in its most impracticable form. Life there is more 'aloof' from the ground-level than in any other forest region. Mr. Ogilvie Grant dwells with due emphasis on this often forgotten 'aspect of Nature' in these regions. He points out that the greater part of the island is covered with dense and lofty forests, many of the trees being over two hundred and forty feet high, while there are no hills or rocks from which the forest can be surveyed. The forest animals, monkeys, lorises, and the like, live at a height of two hundred feet from the ground, that being the 'sunlight level,' below which direct light and heat do not penetrate. Invisible, on the top of this region, live the birds of the tropical forest; and on a still higher aerial plane, also invisible, float the raptorial birds which prey upon them. This 'tree-top' plane of the great forest, being still *terra incognita*, has always been regarded as a possible region in which some great bird or ape may be discovered; and in spite of accumulated difficulties, Mr. Whitehead did make such a discovery. He has found, and brought home from the island, the largest raptorial bird yet discovered, the great forest eagle of Samar.

The discovery of this mighty bird of prey is the more creditable to the explorer because only one pair of the giant eagles was seen. Their haunt was watched daily, and at last the male bird was shot, and though it remained in the top of one of the lofty trees, clinging firmly with its huge claws to the branches, a native climbed to the summit and brought it down. Its weight was judged by Mr. Whitehead at between sixteen and twenty pounds, and being then weakened by fever he could scarcely hold it out at arm's length. Taking the mean of the two weights mentioned as probably correct, the great forest eagle weighs exactly half as much again as the golden eagle, the female of which weighs twelve pounds.

The skin of this bird is now preserved at the Museum of Natural History at South Kensington. As it is the only adult specimen in the world available for inspection by naturalists, it is not exhibited in the public part of the collection, and though the coloured plate by Keulemans which illustrates Mr. Ogilvie Grant's paper is a model of accurate drawing, it does not leave the impression of size given by the skin when actually seen and handled. The *length* of the eagle and the huge size of its beak and claws are the features most striking in the specimen at South Kensington. Like most raptorial birds which seek their prey in woods or forests, from the sparrow-hawk upwards, it has rather short wings in proportion to its great bulk. The tail, on the other hand, is very long. In its equipment for flight and steering it is much like an enormous goshawk. There are two or three such hawks, as large as many of the eagles, half goshawk, half buzzard, which have been found in parts of the tropical forest, though for the reasons mentioned above they are very rarely seen, and still more rarely captured for collections. But in its combined armament of beak and claws the forest eagle exceeds not only all these great hawks, but each and every one of the other eagles. The beak is not larger than that of Pallas's sea eagle, and the power of the wrist and claws is not so great as that of the harpy eagle. But the combination of the two weapons of offence possessed by the Samar eagle is greater than that of either of the formidable species named. The beak is so hooked that the outline in profile is the perfect segment of a circle, the exact centre of which is the point at which the skin, called the cere, joins the cutting edge of the upper mandible. Mr. Grant notes that the depth of the bill is greater than that of any known bird of prey, except Pallas's sea eagle, and it is so compressed that the edges must cut like a double-bladed knife. The skull is very large, much larger than that of the harpy eagle, and the claws and feet are specially adapted for holding large animals with close, thick fur, the length of wrist and close covering of scales giving full play to the talons. The nature of the prey against which this exceptional armament is directed is still matter of conjecture. The natives say that the eagle lives mainly by killing monkeys. This is a very probable statement; there is some evidence from the state of the eagle's skin brought to Europe that it takes its prey on the trees. The quills of several of the wing and tail feathers were broken, 'bearing testimony to many a savage struggle among the branches.' The green macaque is the monkey believed by the people of Samar to be the chief prey of their great eagle. But among the monkeys of these islands are several species of singular size and strength. Even if the great apes of Borneo are not found in Samar, there are probably other species of the monkey tribe, like those found in Java and in the neighbouring islands, which would be most dangerous animals for any bird to attack. No creatures are, for their size, so full of unexpected resources when attacked as the medium-sized and large monkeys. Their arms and hands are surprisingly strong. They can leap instantaneously for a considerable distance without gathering their bodies together for a spring, and their power of biting is that of a bulldog. Against birds they have the power, which they well know how to use, of grasping and breaking a limb, or tearing out the wing or tail feathers. Their habit of combining to rescue one of their fellows makes them still more formidable to animals of prey; and, with the exception of the leopard and the python, most of these agree to let the 'bandur-log' alone. A battle between the great forest eagles and the great forest apes must be one of the heroic episodes of 'high life above stairs' in the jungle, and it may be hoped that when the pacification of the Philippines renders it possible for Mr. Whitehead to revisit the islands, he may bring back some 'field-notes' on the daily life of the new eagle. It is characteristic of the difficulty of making such observations, that though he never saw the bird on the neighbouring island of Leite, he often heard its cry above the tree-tops, and identified it by his experience in Samar. It is also said to be found on the island of Luzon.

Mr. Ogilvie Grant conjectures that the crowned harpy eagle of tropical America is the nearest known ally of the great forest eagle of the Philippines. In this connection it is interesting to note how very little is still known of this other forest eagle. Mr. Salvin, during several years spent in the forests of Central America, only once saw a harpy eagle. Oswald in his 'Birds of America' gives perhaps the fullest account of its habits. The list of its prey shows how formidable a creature it is, and enables us to form some idea of the prowess of the great raptor of Samar. In Mexico the harpy eagle 'kills fawns, sloths, full-grown foxes and badgers, middle-sized pigs, and the black Sapa-jou monkey, whose weight exceeds its own by more than three times.' This last feat may be compared with the natives' statement that the Samar eagle also lives on monkeys.

XXXVIII.—THE PAST AND FUTURE OF BRITISH MAMMALS

A RECENT number of the *Edinburgh Review* contained an interesting essay on our lost and vanishing land mammals. Omitting the seals, whales and porpoises from his list, the writer gave a careful history of the 'last days' of the bear, the wolf, the boar and the beaver in these islands, and an estimate of the future of the wild cat, polecat, marten, otter and badger if the forces which have made for their extermination are unchecked. Of the lost animals, the bears were the first to disappear. They were so numerous that in Roman times Scotch bears were regularly shipped to Rome for use in the arena. One wonders who were employed to catch them, but the urgent requests made to Cicero when Governor of Cilicia to supply his friends in Rome with 'panthers' shows that this was a recognised means of obliging political friends at a much earlier date. The writer notes that the town of Norwich, in the time of Edward the Confessor, used to furnish annually one bear to the King and six dogs to bait it with, and Mr. Lydekker considers that these were possibly native-bred animals. The story of the wolf is admirably told. Among other records quoted is one that all the deer were killed by wolves in Farley Park, in Worcestershire, in the reign of Edward II.; and that a certain Mr. Jonathan Grubb, who was born in 1808, informed Mr. Harting in a letter that his grandmother was born in 1731, and that she remembered her uncle telling her how, in County Kildare, his brother came home on horseback pursued by a pack of wolves, which overtook him and kept leaping on to the hindquarters of his horse until he reached the door. The wild boar outlived the wolf in England. There is a reference to wild boars in Suffolk in the household accounts kept at Hengrave Hall, in Suffolk, in the reign of Henry VIII., and under Elizabeth they remained, together with the half-wild cattle, at Earl Ferrers's castle at Chartley in Staffordshire, in Needwood Forest. We may add that in Fleming's translation of Caius's book on English dogs, written for Gesner, it is mentioned that the ban-dog is 'serviceable to drive *wilde* and tame swyne out of medows, pastures, glebe-landes, and places planted with fruit.' So wild boars were plentiful enough to do mischief in the middle of the sixteenth century.

Which will be the next to disappear? If any

more creatures must follow the bear and the wolf, they are the wild cat, with the marten and polecat following. But it is within the range of probabilities that even the first may be preserved from total extinction for a period not inconsiderable in the history of our islands, though perhaps not appreciable in the duration of a species. That martens had begun to die out in Ireland in the reign of Charles I. is evident from a letter of Lord Strafford's to the Archbishop of Canterbury, which is not quoted in the *Edinburgh*. He promises to send some skins, but adds: 'The truth is, that as the woods decay, so do the hawkes and martens of this kingdom. But in some woods I have, my purpose is, by all means I can, to set up a breed of martens; a good one of these is as much worth as a good wether, yet neither eats so much nor costs so much in attendance. But then the pheasants must look to themselves.' Is not this characteristic of Strafford's modernness and business energy? He adds that, 'standing to get a shoot at a buck, I was so damnably bitten by midges, as my face is all mezled over ever since.' As the *Edinburgh* Reviewer has exhibited great research in tracing the physical causes which have contributed in the past to kill off our larger quadrupeds, it may not be out of place to recall some of the sentimental reasons which in the present tend to prolong the existence of the survivors.

First among these is public feeling, which has recently changed in regard to the preservation of wild animals, as it did a few years earlier in regard to the preservation of our ancient forests. This in turn aids the great proprietors who, both in England and Scotland, protect rare birds and beasts, and even introduce lost species like the beaver. Several Highland owners now protect their wild cats, or give orders that they shall not be destroyed if any wander to their demesnes. The same has been done by Irish proprietors in the case of the marten. Neither are the surviving animals behindhand in taking advantage of the chances given them. Most of them have become astonishingly wary and vigilant after centuries of persecution. They owe their survival to this, and, when matters are made easier for them, do not relax their precautions. The writer of the *Edinburgh* article notes that 'even now very little is known of the habits of our mammals in a wild state.' This is because they have nearly all become intensely nocturnal, and their senses are so acute that no one can watch them closely. The badger's power of hearing is astonishing. Tame specimens have been known to run off and hide five minutes before the arrival of a stranger whose footfall they heard. Foxes which are artificially preserved during part of the year become fairly tame; but even the otters, which are bold and playful animals at night, are quite invisible by day. Some figures from the

Sutherland estates show how numerous some of our carnivora were sixty years ago. In three years from 1831, nine hundred and one wild cats, polecats and martens were killed on the Sutherland estates. Should the present Duke of Sutherland decide to preserve the two first, there is very little doubt that their numbers would recover; and in the deer forests, where grouse and hares are looked upon as a nuisance, there is no reason why this should not be done. Another and more hopeful fact in the present state of our wild animal population is that two of the largest are far more common than is believed. Otters are numerous, and badgers by no means scarce. Many proprietors protect the badger; others have reintroduced it, Sir Herbert Maxwell, in Wigtownshire, among the number. As badgers never ' show,' this is a public-spirited action; but there is no adequate reason why the badger should not enjoy the benefit of a few years' absolute protection under a special Act of Parliament. It deserves this, because the badgers are now purposely killed to make pouches for the Highlanders. 'The year 1842 was a bad one for the poor badgers, owing to the revival of Highland dress after the Queen's visit.' Those delightful beasts, the otters, are, we are glad to say, increasingly common in England itself, and in no danger of extermination. On little streams, where they kill trout, they are killed themselves. But by most of

OTTER ON LAKE SIDE.

our deep rivers, notably the Thames, and nearly all its tributaries, the Norfolk Broads and rivers, and almost all the largest streams of Southern England, they are quite common and increase. Evidence of this is shown by the way in which otters have recently turned up in all sorts of unexpected places, even on the smallest feeders of Thames tributary streams, and on ornamental lakes remote from rivers. Some very small brooks which rise in the chalk downs and run into the little river Ock, which in turn joins the Thames at Abingdon, have lately been artificially stocked with trout, at their headwaters in the sides of the hills. On two adjacent streams of this kind otters appeared, and made havoc among the fish. Fourteen traps were set along a chain of pools to catch one of the invaders, but he escaped them all. On a lake in a very waterless district of Essex, far from any considerable stream, otters also appeared, and have taken up their abode. They kill numbers of large carp, and by the skeletons of the carp a number of shells of fresh-water mussels, with the ends bitten out, are generally found. The otters like mussel-sauce with their fish, but will also eat the mussels alone. On the whole length of the Thames itself, from Gloucestershire to Hampton Court, otters live and flourish, hunting only at night, and then entirely concealed by the deep water. The skeletons of the fish they eat are the index of their presence.

Failing the rivers, there is another favourite haunt of otters, which time can hardly destroy. This is among the cliffs on the sea coast. They are quite at home in salt water, and in Devonshire there are probably quite as many sea otters as river otters.

The most to be regretted of our lost animals is the beaver. The records of its extinction are very meagre, and there does not seem any reason why a few might not have survived in forest areas, such as the Forest of Dean, or those of Northern Scotland, to a later date than that of Richard Cœur de Lion, when Giraldus Cambrensis recorded their existence on the river Teifi. Beavers lived on the river Kennet, near Newbury, for a beaver's jaw was found there in the peat; and on the Severn there is a beaver island. But as the price of a Welsh beaver's skin was fifteen times more than that of otter's skin in 940 A.D., they must have been scarce even at that date. It is interesting to know, from Sir Edmund Loder's continued success with his beavers at Leonardslee, that we can, if we like, re-establish them. The Leonardslee beavers increase, and have continued to do so for nine years. As they destroy much small timber, no one who regards cost would encourage them on a small estate or among valuable trees. But the beavers have two ways of life, differing according to the rivers on which they live, as may be seen in Northern Norway. Shallow streams they *dam;* and to make this dam they cut down trees and do mischief. But on deep, slow streams, such as the Thames, they make burrows in the bank and 'lodges,' but do not attempt to build dams, because the water is deep enough for their wants. All they need is enough willow-bark to feed on. If anyone would turn out a few beavers on the Thames, and let them have the run of an osier-bed, they would probably increase and multiply.

XXXIX.—THE RETURN OF THE GREAT BUSTARD

A SMALL flock of great bustards, temporarily kept at the Zoo, was recently imported from Spain, and one or more pairs of these birds were, it was said, to be turned out on an old haunt of the species on the Yorkshire Wolds. It is not so much matter for surprise that the restoration of this, the largest of our native birds, is about to be attempted now, but that it has not been tried earlier, and on a larger scale. It would be unsafe to assume that because the capercailzie now flourishes in the Scotch woods, the permanent restoration of the bustard to its ancient haunts on the Wiltshire Downs, the Wolds, and the Norfolk heaths and 'brecks' is equally possible. But though some species refuse utterly to acquiesce in change either of habit or environment, and, like the black tern, the avocet, and the bartailed godwit, migrate to seek elsewhere what they no longer find in this country, there is good reason to believe that there is no such obstacle to the return of the bustard.

Anyone willing to spend money and trouble on such an experiment would wish to know whether the bird is found flourishing elsewhere in conditions like those in which it would find itself in the England of to-day; and secondly, whether the causes which led to its final disappearance here were permanent or accidental. Fortunately, there is a very interesting and reliable body of evidence on both these points in the bustard's history. Both the late Lord Lilford and Mr. Abel Chapman attentively studied the haunts and habits of the bustard in Spain; and the late Mr. Stevenson delayed for a long time the publication of his second volume of 'The Birds of Norfolk' to write a complete, and incidentally most charming, account of the facts connected with the 'decline and fall' of the same birds in their last home in Norfolk. There was no authority, from Mr. Alfred Newton to the 'shepherd's pages' of Icklingham Heath, from whom Mr. Stevenson did not gather facts first hand as to the disappearance of our largest bird. And the inference from his account is, with one exception, not unfavourable to its restoration.

At present it is an exceedingly common bird in Southern Spain. Its numbers are probably reinforced by migrants from the higher and colder central districts of La Mancha and Old Castile; but it also remains there throughout the year, in the midst of high cultivation, and maintains itself, by its own wary habits, without legal protection, amongst a population who are very ready to kill it by any means, however unsportsmanlike. Some of these devices are almost identical with those used in Norfolk, water in hot weather taking the place of corn or turnips as a bait for the birds, which are shot from ambush. To the fair sportsman it offers the opportunity of stalking it with a rifle, or 'driving'; for though slow to rise it has a powerful flight, and the stories of its former capture in this country by means of greyhounds are generally discredited. Lord Lilford has seen them within sight of the Giralda of Seville from the beginning of February till the end of September. ' In February flocks, varying in number from eight or ten to sixty or more, are to be seen on all the pasture and corn lands of the district, especially on the right of the Guadalquivir, a few miles above Seville, a country of rolling down-land, for the most part under cultivation.' This ground very closely corresponds with the conditions of most of the Berkshire and Wiltshire Downs, and is more highly cultivated than that part of Salisbury Plain which is passing into the hands of the War Office. The birds are so far from disliking cultivated land that they nest in the young wheat in the great alluvial plains of the lower Guadalquivir, just as they did by preference in the young rye in Norfolk. They usually do not lay more than two or sometimes three eggs, and nest early, at the end of April. The eggs are thus liable to be destroyed when the corn is rolled, or taken by the labourers employed in hoeing, risks more common, probably, in this country than in Spain. While the hen birds are sitting in the corn, the male bustards stalk about in the cattle pastures. 'Many of these fields barely afford sufficient covert to conceal a lark; here these splendid birds may be observed in all their glory of perfect nuptial plumage, and conscious strength and beauty, stalking about with a stealthy and deliberate gait, and showing off, apparently from pure pride of life, in turkey-cock fashion.'

A cleverly-stuffed cock bustard at the Natural History Museum at South Kensington shows this curious nuptial display of the bird. It is a very large male, which weighed 37 lb., and was presented by Mr. Abel Chapman. The head is buried in the neck, which is greatly inflated; the 'beard' is brought up on either side of the head; and the tail and wings seem to have been turned inside out and arranged over its back. Beneath the outer brown and black feathers are beautifully-curved pure white ones, both in wings and tail, which cover the whole of the back, as if arranged by a feather-dresser. Lord Lilford's experiences may be supplemented from some interesting

chapters in Messrs. Abel Chapman and W. J. Buck's
'Wild Spain.' It is evident that the birds are just as
much at home, and as well able to take care of themselves, as are partridges in this country, on the 'vast
stretches of silent corn-land' which are the Spanish
bustard's home. 'Among the objects of sport there are
few more attractive scenes than a band of bustards at
rest. Bring your field-glasses to bear on that gathering which you see yonder, basking in the sunshine, in
the full enjoyment of their siesta. There are four or
five and twenty of them; and how immense they look
against the background of sprouting corn which covers
the landscape; a stranger might well mistake them for
deer or goats. Most of the birds are sitting turkey-fashion, their heads sunk among their feathers; others
stand in drowsy yet half-suspicious attitudes, their broad
backs resplendent with those mottled hues of true
game-colour, and their lavender necks and well-poised
heads contrasting with the snowy whiteness of their
lower plumage.' This is a sketch largely from the
sportsman's point of view; but as sportsmen are likely
to take a prominent share in the coming restoration of
the bird, those who are not familiar with this description
may derive some encouragement from such an agreeable
picture. 'Driving bustards' is evidently an exciting
and artistic form of sport, and the birds, except the old
cocks, are excellent for the table. It is evident that in

Spain they are not averse to modern cultivation; in fact, they prefer the corn-lands. The story o. their disappearance in Norfolk shows that, far from disliking corn-land, they were only too fond of it. They would lay their eggs in the winter-sown wheat, which is high and green early in spring. When wheat began to be drilled and hoed, instead of being sown broadcast, every bustard's nest was found. Though forbidden by the Act of 25 Henry VIII., these eggs were taken by the farm boys and labourers, and kept as curiosities or eaten. As there were only two 'droves' left early in the present century—one in the open country round Swaffham, the other near Thetford, of which the former only numbered twenty-seven in or about the year 1820, while after the year 1812 the Thetford 'drove' was only reckoned at twenty-four—it is not strange that with constant 'egging' and occasional shooting they disappeared. The last nest in Norfolk was probably that made on a farm at Great Massingham in 1835 or 1836, from which some eggs were taken, one of which is preserved. The destruction of the eggs and killing of the birds is clearly within the limits of prevention; and no County Council would refuse a resolution to enforce the law, which still exists, against the taking of bustards' eggs. The bird, its eggs, and young, are already protected by Section 24 of the Game Act or 1831, which also gives it a close season from March 1 to September 1, and makes a license necessary to kill it, and trespass in its pursuit an offence under the Act. There remains the question whether any change in the surface of the country has taken place which might render their old haunts less acceptable to the birds. The answer is in the negative, *except* in the case of those very parts of Norfolk in which it lingered latest. This region, known as the 'breck' district, was subject to constant sandstorms, and the blowing sand cut and injured the young wheat. To stop this belts of trees were planted, and its open character changed. This, Mr. Stevenson considered, 'rendered it entirely unsuitable to the wary habits of the bustard.' But the whole of the Berkshire and Wiltshire Downs, the Wolds of Yorkshire and Lincolnshire, and much of the Fen district, is still ideal ground for the bird. It must be remembered that the bustard, though resident formerly all the year in England, is potentially migratory. Stray birds do occasionally appear still from overseas, one of the last being seen in the Fens. Lord Lilford obtained a mate for this bird, but it died one cold night after it was liberated, and the cock bird then disappeared.

It was never suggested as a cause of its disappearance that the bustard was destroyed as destructive to crops or a nuisance to the farmer. In Spain its diet varies at different seasons. For animal food it likes frogs, mice, lizards, earth-worms, snails, beetles, locusts, and grasshoppers; the latter it devours with particular relish. Its taste in vegetables is less to the farmer's liking. It eats green corn, especially barley, clover, the leaves of mallow, chick-peas, and vetches. In Norfolk its food was much the same, with the substitution of turnip-tops for chick-peas ; it also ate seeds of weeds and the leaves of colewort and dandelion. Everyone will hope that the return of the bustard will not long be delayed, and that those who undertake its restoration may meet with ready and willing help from their neighbours, rich and poor. It is probable that it never was, and never will be, very numerous as a species. But public interest is alive to subjects of this kind at present, and the moment is favourable for the attempt.

XL.—BIG GAME

A CIRCULAR was lately issued to sportsmen, inviting them to join in a big-game shooting expedition to British East Africa. The particular district selected as a hunting-ground was that round Mount Kenia, the route being viâ Mombasa and the Uganda railway. The advertised cost for twelve months was three hundred pounds, which leaves rather a narrow margin for contingencies ; and of the big game which figured among the probable bag, one, the quagga, is extinct, and another, the spring-buck, is not found north of the Zambesi. But there is no doubt whatever that in spite of the decrease of most big game in its old haunts, there is in Cape Colony, the Transvaal, Natal, the Northern States of America, and some parts of Arctic Europe, notably in Spitzbergen, abundance of sport left, and sport of an unusual kind, accessible at a moderate cost, and with no great loss of time on the journey. Of the hunting-grounds of the future we say something later. But at the present moment the noblest trophies of the rifle may be secured both in South Africa and East Africa, in India, and in North America, further afield, it is true, than in the past, but not further in point of time. Africa, for instance, affords three main areas open to big-game shooters— Mashonaland, East Central Africa, and Somaliland. Of these, Mashonaland is accessible by rail, either viâ Mafeking or by Beira, and the Uganda railway will soon open up the northern district.

Portuguese South-East Africa also swarms with game. The list of large animals exceeds thirty species, including lions, leopards, cheetah, hippopotamus, ostrich, sable-antelope, water-buck, koodoo, pallah, hartbeest, bison, tsesseby, and many other of the finest game animals in Africa. Somaliland is another, and perhaps the favourite, haunt of the modern big-game shooter in Africa. There he finds a hotter climate, and even better, though more expensive, sport; for camels must be hired, and a large retinue maintained. Elephant, black rhinoceros, and numbers of zebra of two species, as well as a vast list of antelope, are to be found and killed by any well-managed expedition. India seems almost to be forgotten by big-game shooters leaving England, and left to residents. Yet Indian sport has on the whole rather expanded in kind and quality than diminished. To the 'old-fashioned' sport of our grandfathers, the splendid jungle-shooting recorded in such books as that best of Indian sporting novels, 'The Old Forest Ranger,' or the diaries of General Douglas Hamilton and his brother 'Hawkeye,' is now added the mountain-shooting of thur, ibex, and all the varieties of wild goats and wild sheep. But the 'old-fashioned' animals still abound. A writer in *Country Life*, describing big-game shooting in Berar, states that in one district there were such numbers of cheetul deer, wild hog, and other game, that the tigers, which also abounded, would scarcely condescend to kill a bullock when tied up for their especial benefit. Bears are also numerous wherever there are hills; so are the great bison in half a dozen of the great forest districts, and sambur, swamp-deer, leopards, buffalo, ibex, and nilgai in suitable country.

The ambition of the modern big-game hunter is to return with a mixed set of trophies, not a series of the same kind. Consequently he is not content with a whole season's 'still hunting' in the Canadian forest, when the first light snow has fallen, and moose and cariboo can be followed with surroundings and equipment unchanged since the days of Montcalm, because he can *only* get moose and cariboo, or black-tailed deer or mule-deer. The climate and surroundings are almost perfect; and he can have this sport mixed with canoeing, rough fishing, and plenty of small-game shooting when he likes. But what he desires is, if in North

America, a varied and striking collection of hides and horns, skins of the grizzly bear and black bear, horns of the wapiti, moose, cariboo, black-tailed deer, Rocky Mountain goat, and big-horn sheep, and for this he must go further afield, to the magnificent mountain forests and lakes of North British Columbia. It does not matter whether he seeks his sport there or in South Africa, in Khama's country, in Mashonaland, in the Upper Zambesi, or in India. In any of these fields he can amass those magnificent sets of trophies which are now seen in so many sportsmen's homes, and form, merely in transit between the packing-case and the country house, a permanent collection always changing, but never growing less, in the establishments of one or two first-class taxidermists and mounters of skins and horns. The size and splendour of some of these trophies surpass anything seen in museums, except in that of Mr. Walter Rothschild at Tring. The mere bulk of some of the animals passes belief, and the magnificence of the furs and horns makes the average Englishman wildly covetous to obtain something himself which shall match them.

As mere instances of the size of the trophies, we may take, for example, the gigantic elephant's head at Tring, with tusks nine feet long. There is, of course, another side to this quest for trophies. The writer has seen at one of the great taxidermist's the newly-tanned and bullet-pierced skin of a lion spread out for inspection before the brother of the man whom it had killed the instant after it received its death-wound. But fatal accidents are increasingly rare in modern big-game shooting. The rifles are accurate, not too heavy, and frightfully destructive; and very many of the noted big-game hunters are marvellous shots. Those who doubt it should watch the shooting of such great hunters as Mr. Littledale or Sir E. G. Loder when firing double shots at the 'running deer' at Bisley, and putting, not once, but twice, thrice, or four times, two bullets, right and left, into a moving target no larger than a breakfast plate. Fortunately for the big-game hunter, there are new regions opening out for him even now. There is every reason to believe that one of these will offer almost the finest sport, and of the most satisfactory kind yet found, except, perhaps, in the days of the early lion-hunters in South Africa. The scene is the valley of the Upper Amoor, and its great tributary the Ussuri. On the former, bear, boar, and the magnificent maral stag abound, in some of the most beautiful scenery, and one of the best climates, in the world. The Lower Amoor is 'feverish,' except in winter; but the valley of the Ussuri river, which joins the Amoor at the point where the latter turns due north, and forms the boundary between Chinese Manchuria and the Russian coast province, holds the finest beast of prey in the world, the Northern or Siberian tiger. No one quite knows to what dimensions the Siberian tiger will *not* grow. One owned by Mr. Hagenbeck was a far larger animal than he or any other had ever seen either alive or represented by its skin. The coat is immensely long in winter, of a rich dark orange, with an undergrowth of fur, and makes an incomparable trophy. Both these Northern tigers and bears were recently so plentiful on the Ussuri, that the Russian Government offered a large reward for their destruction, and gave every encouragement to the officers of the East Siberian army to go and hunt there. But Russian officers have not that passion for sport which seems inbred in Englishmen abroad, and recent accounts state that the ravages made among the cattle of the new Russian settlers are still a most serious drawback to colonization. The wild boars of the Ussuri are also very fine animals. There are two of these at the Tring museum, but they do not equal the dimensions of the huge European boar from the Carpathians recently exhibited at the International Fur Store. This European boar, shot within a few days by rail from London, weighed six hundred and twenty pounds, beating the record of the chestnut-fed boars of the Caucasus. Its bristles were so wiry, long, and thick, that they looked like a piece of rough heather thatching.

Before the East Siberian hunting-field is developed, another will probably be once more open to the British big-game hunter. This is the Kassala district and the valley of the Atbara river, which before its occupation by the Dervishes was absolutely the finest sporting-ground left in Africa. It was the land of the 'hunting Arabs,' very healthy, abounding in water and cover, and the home *par excellence* of the black rhinoceros, the lion, and smaller African carnivora of many species, large antelope, and, in places, of the elephant and giraffe. It is believed that an immense increase of wild animals has recently taken place there, partly because the population has been too harassed by the triangular war between Dervishes, Abyssinians, and Italians to kill off the game, and partly because the famous tribe of sword-hunters, the Hamran Arabs, were nearly exterminated twelve years ago by an epidemic. The Klondike discoveries will give, indirectly, better facilities for reaching North British Columbia and Southern Alaska than have hitherto been available, and though not 'new' hunting-grounds, they will come within range of a much larger number of sportsmen. The forest region of the Black Sea coast of the Caucasus will probably remain, as it is at present, the home of great quantities of big game, but an impossible hunting-ground. The valleys are full of fever; diphtheria seems native to the soil; and though bear, boar, and deer abound, leopards are not uncommon, and one or the remaining herds of European bison still remains there. The forest is so thick, so wet, and so unhealthy, that it cannot become a regular hunting-ground. There remains one more possible new hunting-ground, the oldest in the world, for it was possibly the scene of Nimrod's own exploits. This is the Baghtiara highlands of Persia, where the lion is still numerous by the thick covers near the rivers. The late Sir Henry Laird, when a guest of these mountain tribes, was informed that all the black-maned lions were not only good Mussulmans, but 'Shiahs' to a lion, and only required the name of Hassan and Hosein to be mentioned if they were required to move on. The yellow-maned lions were 'Kaffirs,' and were shot at sight.

XLI.—GAME PRESERVATION IN THE UNITED STATES

At the present moment one of the burning questions of domestic interest in the United States is the enactment of Game Laws. The origin of the movement is curiously unlike that from which similar legislation sprang in this country, though its object is identical. In the various States of the Union the public are clamouring for game preservation and stricter supervision, while private owners are, if anything, rather in opposition to the general wish. Sport is the main object of the new desire for game preservation, but æsthetic feelings are not without influence, and the legislators who desire penalties for wearing wild birds' feathers act in harmony with those who wish to enact more stringent Game Laws. The activities of these reformers are so numerous, and spread over a country of such vast area, that it is difficult to present them in any continuous scheme; but we give some of the questions of the hour to illustrate the energy of this spontaneous and democratic movement in favour of State protection of game. Its intensely popular and local character is shown by the fact that every separate State is now enforcing existing Game Laws or adding to their number. Dakota, Illinois, Tennessee, New York, Maine, Vermont, and many others, are engaged in revising or adding to these laws, which are enforced not by private persons, but by State gamekeepers. In Maine, for instance, though so near to the great cities of the East, sportsmen are expected to use the services of licensed guides, who are really State 'gillies.' Strict close time is enforced, and these men have the protection of game and fish mainly in their control throughout the territory. But the State 'game warden' is also a recognised institution. His exploits in catching poachers are chronicled with enthusiasm in the Press, in a very different tone to that often adopted when poachers are summoned before British magistrates. Under the heading of 'Arrests in Montana,' we find that 'a partial check has been given to the elk butchers' by summary arrests; that wholesale skin-hunters' camps have been raided by the constables, and the offenders put in gaol; and that 'warrants are out for two prominent citizens,' no less personages than a State senator and a schoolmaster. Endless complaints, informations, and prosecutions for killing deer in close time, occupy the columns of the local papers. If half the grumbling on this subject appeared in the columns of the *Field* and *Country Life* which is inserted weekly in the New York *Forest and Stream*, there would be a popular outcry against over-preservation. Curious complications arise from these laws. As each State preserves its own game, and pays its own wardens, it naturally objects to citizens of other States shooting in its forests without contribution or domicile. Consequently, certain States imposed shooting licenses on non-residents from other States. The latter then complained that this was a breach of the American Constitution, which secures equal rights to all citizens in all States alike. An action was brought against the State of Connecticut by a citizen, but the State won. So in the Supreme Court of California it was laid down that 'the wild game within a State belongs to the people in their collective capacity. It is not the subject of private ownership, except in so far as the people may elect to make it so, and they may, if they see fit, absolutely prohibit the taking of it or traffic or commerce in it, if it is deemed necessary for protection or preservation.' This judgment thus does not forbid private ownership, but asserts State ownership in general. As a matter of fact, private ownership of game does exist in many States, and makes such places as the Corbin Park possible. Shooting licenses will probably be made compulsory on 'outsiders' by the States whose sporting rights they desire to enjoy. A recent meeting at Chicago with the object of enforcing game protection in the State of Illinois elicits the following comments in a leading paper, which gives the modern American views on game preserving in a form not more exalted than is commonly seen in the discussion of such topics: 'Altogether aside from the consideration of game as a food resource is the influence it has upon the health and stamina of the race. This is not in any degree a fanciful view of the supply of wild game as a public benefit, and game protection as a public charge. It has had recognition from early days, and has furnished reason for the enactment and enforcement of Game Laws. The whole country reaps advantage when its public men seek the woods for their recreations; the community shares the good which its citizens find in camp and field. Game is a public property; those appointed to protect it are the trustees of the public; game protection is a public trust.' This public trust is occasionally exercised to private detriment. Thus in Long Island, at thirty miles from New York, deer are so numerous, in consequence of the prohibition of hunting with hounds as well as shooting, that the market-gardeners' bitter cry is now being heard. One of these writes a furious letter of complaint, of which the following extracts are somewhat amusing.

Perhaps even stronger language would be used were the market-gardens in Gunnersbury or Fulham. 'The depredations on all kinds of truck are fearful, and drive the small farmers, who especially suffer, to madness and despondency. Ask, for example, the people of Bohemianville how they have to suffer, despite all precautions, by putting up scarecrows, hanging out lanterns, etc., to keep off the deer. In making such an onerous Game Law, the State expropriates the farmer without giving him compensation ; the State takes the food out of the toiler's mouth and gives it to the deer.' After remarking that, instead of encouraging the growing of vegetables to supply the poor with cheap food, 'the State goes to breeding wild animals,' the writer adds that, when trying to get compensation from the Board of Supervisors, the Board answered humorously that the farmers 'should start a revolution.' 'Is that equal rights?' asks this citizen of Long Island. In Maine a difficulty of an unforeseen kind is urged against modern State preservation. By the old laws of the colony of Massachusetts, the founders of this refuge for tender consciences enacted that no game preservation should be permitted, and further declared that the right of free fishing and fowling should pertain to all on any great pond containing more than ten acres of water, and that the right to pass and repass to any such water should remain for ever unabridged, providing that the persons using it did not trespass upon any man's corn or meadow.' This statute was upheld in a recent judgment, and a newly-made private game-park was thrown open to the public. An odd phase of the present keenness of the public for public sport is the attack recently made on cold storage solely because it makes the detection of breakers of the close season more difficult by preserving game all the year round in condition for market. It was seriously alleged that cold storing of game made it poisonous, or, at least, unfit for human food. The subject was discussed at immense length, and the adversaries of cold storage were the *popular* party in the dispute, the thinness of the arguments being backed up by the goodness of the cause, which was not solicitude for wholesome food, but for the protection of game in close time.

The men who kill winged game in the close season make immense bags in many districts, and by supplying unscrupulous owners of cold stores with grouse, wild geese, quail, and wild-fowl, earn large sums, and do much mischief. The following specimen of a Yankee poacher's letter, offering to make himself useful in this way, was recently forwarded by the recipient to the *Forest and Stream.* The spelling is given *literatim :* 'jenuarry the 28. Mr —— i hav Bin sicK for fower weeks SinCe i saw your agent. i am gittin game rite now i have some gees i will sent them in now mr i will do business with you i will sent you som eggs. how long can you Handel Birds privetly mr send priCes onCe a weak is anuf.' The game chiefly preserved in the old States are black-tailed deer, Virginian deer, wild duck, and other fowl, Californian quail, sage hens, and ruffed grouse. Bears and foxes benefit by the close season extended to game. Westwards the big game of the Rocky Mountains, wapiti (or 'elk'), wild-sheep, wild-goats, and winged game are also protected in a close season settled by the different States. Both Virginian deer and, in the State of Maine, the woodland cariboo and other deer have much increased of recent years. The latest development of this democratic game preserving is the introduction of the English pheasant. Private persons began and succeeded in the experiments; but now certain States have taken to pheasant preserving; the first sets of eggs and subsequent broods have been reared in State pheasantries and protected by rigorous laws for a period of five years.

The whole movement is a curious illustration of the intense Anglo-Saxon love of sport, and of the sense of fair play due to game which marks the distinction between sport and the commercial killing of game. It would not be possible in a country which did not, as the United States, abound in wild 'unimproved' land, forests, and swampy rivers. In time, as the population grows, the game must diminish in spite of State protection. But for the present the Americans are determined that no such waste of animal life by unrestricted shooting shall recur as that which destroyed the bison, and has reduced to a few individuals the largest flocks of any species of bird ever seen in one place, the once innumerable colonies of passenger-pigeons.

XLII.—ANIMAL ACCLIMATIZATION AT WOBURN ABBEY

THIS volume, which began with an instance of the necessity for animals to-day, shown in the demand for the reindeer and snow-camel for Klondike, may close appropriately with a significant example of the value set on animals as among the pleasures of life.

During recent years the Duke of Bedford has carried out a scheme of animal acclimatization in the park at Woburn Abbey on a scale never before attempted in this country. Birds as well as quadrupeds are the subjects of this experiment, and the magnificent pheasants of India and China haunt the woods in large numbers. But the greater number of the animals are various kinds of deer, of which no fewer than thirty-four species are in the open park or paddocks—bison, zebras, antelopes, wild sheep and goats, and yaks. The novelty and freshness of this experiment consists not only in the accumulation of such a number of species, interesting as this is to the naturalist, but in their way of life, free and unconfined in an English park. That is the lot of the greater number of the animals at Woburn, some being entirely free and wandering at large, like the native red-deer and fallow-deer, while the others, though for the present in separate enclosures, are kept in reserves so spacious, and so lightly though effectively separated, that they have the appearance of enjoying the same degree of liberty. Almost the first question which suggests itself is, What is the general effect of this gathering of over-sea animals, from the African veldt and Indian hills, the Manchurian mountains and North American prairies, and from wild-animal land *quod ubique est*, on the green pastures and under the elms and oaks round the home of a great English family? Briefly, we may say that the effect is magnificent. On leaving Woburn, the valleys and meadows stocked with our ordinary domestic animals seem solitary and deserted after the eye has rested for hours on the varied and impressive forms that crowd the slopes, groves, and glades of this fine park. This effect is due in part to the largeness of the scale on which the stocking of Woburn with wild animals has been carried out. In the phrase of the farmer, the park 'carries a larger head' of animals than is commonly seen on a similar area, even in the richest pastures. The scene recalls the descriptions of the early travellers in Southern

Africa, when the large fauna roamed there in unbroken numbers, and with little fear of man. The *coup d'œil* in parts of the park where the animals gather thickest is so striking that the mind descends reluctantly to the identification of the species, or to details of dates, origin, and management. From one position, looking up a long green slope towards the Abbey, there could be seen at the time of the writer's last visit between two and three hundred animals, both birds and beasts, feeding or sleeping within sight of the immediate front of the spectator. These varied in species from cranes, storks, and almost every known species of swan, to wapiti stags, antelopes, and zebras, walking, sitting, galloping, feeding, or sleeping. For quite half a mile up the slope the white swans and other wild fowl were dotted among the deer and other ruminants, presenting a strange and most attractive example of the real 'paradise' which animals will make for themselves when only the 'good beasts' are selected to live together. The creatures in this animal Arcadia were grouped nearly as follows. In the foreground was a large pool, circular, with clayey banks, one of a chain of ponds of all sizes, from that of a fishpond to a large lake which lies lower in the park. On and around this pool were many species of swans, and eight of foreign geese; but the greater number of these were scattered, as we have said, over some hundred acres of

An English-bred Gazelle.

park. In the centre of the pond sat a cormorant, and on the grass by the margin some gigantic cranes with crimson heads and gray wings were running and 'dancing' in honour of the sun. On the hill to the left, where the Abbey lies, were five distinct herds or deer. Three of these were fallow bucks and does. One herd was of red-deer, and hybrids between the red-deer and the wapiti. On the sky-line were a herd of pure-bred wapiti, with three huge stags, their horns just cleaned from the velvet. In the centre slope, in diminishing perspective till they appeared mere dots among the trees, were mixed groups of Japanese deer, the same breed which have thriven so remarkably in the parks of Sir Edmund Loder and Lord Powerscourt, fallow bucks and does, red-deer, both 'red' and pure white, of which variety the park holds a considerable number, a few other and smaller foreign deer, and a group of five nylghau antelopes from India. Three of these were reddish-gray in colour, while two were real 'blue bulls,' very fine upstanding beasts, well suited to woodland scenery. On the right, within a hundred yards, lying down or feeding under an ancient elm, was a small herd of zebras, as quiet and at their ease as so many New Forest ponies with their foals. Picture this animal population among the groves and ancient timber of an English park in May. And this is but one among many such sights visible in this unique paradise. The park is high and undulating, with a number of rounded hillocks and elevations. In consequence of the persistent downfall of rain, and the wetness of the pasture, the animals had betaken themselves to the high ground ; and there on the sky-line were seen outlined forms so familiar, yet so strange in their setting, that the visitor might almost incline to doubt whether he were in possession of his waking senses or dreaming of pictures in Catlin's 'North American Indians.' On one hill, for instance, lay sleeping four American bison and a herd of wapiti-deer. The round, humped outlines of the former were seen across a great space of grass, for here the park was treeless, and the animals, though confined in large enclosures of some twenty acres each, looked exactly as they must have appeared before the days of their destruction on the rolling prairies of the North-West.

The mixture of species, far from being incongruous, is most effective. Close by a long avenue of chestnut-trees in blossom was a chance gathering of animals from the Highlands of Scotland and from far Thibet. Four or five small herds of red deer were feeding, mingled with some thirty or forty splendid Highland cattle of all colours, with rough shaggy coats and long horns. Some were black, some red, some smoke-coloured, some of the pinkish-gray seen in soap-stone and in the shaggy coats of these light-coloured moorland cattle. In the centre of these creatures, which were scattered feeding over many acres of ground, was a herd of fourteen yaks. One white-and-gray bull, whose coat touched the ground, led the herd. The rest were black-and-white, cows and calves mingled, feeding or sleeping under the chestnut-trees.

The creatures which roam absolutely free in this great park represent those in the final or perfect state in this animal paradise. But, like the souls in Virgil's land of the just, these happy creatures pass through various stages of probation. Some never reach the stage of complete liberty, or are physically unsuited for complete surrender to outdoor life in England. Many spend part of their time in wide enclosed paddocks contained in the park itself, and are promoted later to wander free and unrestrained.

'Exinde per amplum
Mittimur Elysium et pauci læta arva tenemus,'

might be the motto of these 'dwellers on the threshold.' Life in these paddocks is, in its turn, intermediate between freedom in the open park and the confinement of smaller enclosures, which reproduce on a very ample scale the features of an ideal 'Zoo.' One of these enclosures is a warm walled meadow, with a few old apple-trees in it, such as often lies adjacent to a farm. It was a kind of annexe to the home farm buildings. In it are pools for wild fowl, while rows of farm buildings, now occupied by various birds and beasts which need rest after long journeys by sea and rail, abut on the paddock. In the latter a colony of Patagonian cavies burrow under the apple trees, and pretty little kangaroos, or rather 'wallabies,' with their young in their pouches, hop about in the grass, or lie basking like cats by the side of the water. One wallaby sat upright on the bank, leaning its back against a tree. Its young one, looking out of its pouch, was seriously gazing at its own diminutive features reflected in the water. Brilliant purple gallinules, Patagonian rails, Indian ducks, and pelicans were on the water, and a newly-arrived brood of Japanese teal were resting after their journey in one of the sheds. An interesting feature in this paddock, one which is constantly observable at Woburn, is the friendliness of the various creatures with each other. Some very fine sing-sing antelopes, a dwarf Indian bull, and some Chinese water-deer were associated with the kangaroos and cavies in perfect amity. But this seems characteristic of the place. We noticed a pair of tame deer lying under the single cedar-tree which stands in the great quadrangle made by stables and coachhouses at the back of the main block of Woburn Abbey. A stable-cat, being in want of society, strolled out and sat down exactly between these two deer. As they did not object, the cat got up and rubbed itself against the back of one of the reclining hinds. This is a real 'paradise' at the close of the nineteenth century, and of its kind is among the things best worth seeing in rural England.

THE END

NEW PUBLICATIONS.

TOM TUG AND OTHERS. Sketches in a Domestic Menagerie. By Mrs. DEW SMITH, Author of 'Confidences of an Amateur Gardener.' With Illustrations by ELINOR M. MONSELL. Crown 8vo., 6s.

GEORGE MORLAND, AND THE EVOLUTION FROM HIM OF SOME LATER PAINTERS. By J. T. NETTLESHIP. With Six Copper Plates and many Illustrations printed in sepia. Super royal 8vo. Price 6s. net.

THE WAR IN THE PENINSULA. By ALEXANDER INNES SHAND, Author of 'The Life of Sir Edward Hamley.' With Four Portraits on Copper and Six Plans. 5s.

AFRICA IN THE NINETEENTH CENTURY. By EDGAR SANDERSON, M.A., Author of 'The British Empire,' etc. With Four Portraits on Copper and a Map. 5s.

'Alike interesting as a story, and instructive as a chronicle of important political and international movements.'—*Daily Mail.*

HEROES OF CHIVALRY AND ROMANCE: BEOWULF, ARTHUR, AND SIEGFRIED. By the Rev. A. J. CHURCH. With Eight Illustrations in Colour by G. MORROW. 5s.

THE KING'S REEVE, AND HOW HE SUPPED WITH HIS MASTER. An Old-World Comedy. By the Rev. E. GILLIAT, Author of 'In Lincoln Green.' With Illustrations by SYDNEY HALL. 5s.

'A quaint and interesting picture of life in the reign of Edward I.'—*Scotsman.*

THE ISLAND OF THE ENGLISH. A Story of Napoleon's Days. By FRANK COWPER, Author of 'Caedwalla,' 'The Captain of the Wight,' etc. With Illustrations by GEORGE MORROW. 5s.

'A rattling story of old seafaring and naval days.'—*Academy.*

UNDER THE DOME OF ST. PAUL'S, IN THE DAYS OF SIR CHRISTOPHER WREN. A Story. By Mrs. MARSHALL. With Illustrations by T. HAMILTON CRAWFORD. 5s.

LONDON: SEELEY AND CO., LTD., 38 GREAT RUSSELL ST.

EVENTS OF OUR OWN TIME.

A Series of Volumes on the most Important Events of the last Half-Century, each containing 300 pages or more, in large crown 8vo., with Plans, Portraits, or other Illustrations, to be issued at intervals, price 5s., cloth.

THE LIBERATION OF ITALY. By the Countess MARTINENGO CESARESCO. With Portraits on Copper.

THE WAR IN THE CRIMEA. By General Sir EDWARD HAMLEY, K.C.B. With Five Maps and Plans, and Four Portraits on Copper. Seventh Edition.

THE INDIAN MUTINY OF 1857. By Colonel MALLESON, C.S.I. With Three Plans, and Four Portraits on Copper. Sixth Edition.

THE AFGHAN WARS OF 1839-1842 AND 1878-1880. By ARCHIBALD FORBES. With Five Maps and Plans, and Four Portraits on Copper. Third Edition.

THE REFOUNDING OF THE GERMAN EMPIRE. By Colonel MALLESON, C.S.I. With Five Maps and Plans, and Four Portraits on Copper.

ACHIEVEMENTS IN ENGINEERING DURING THE LAST HALF-CENTURY. By Professor VERNON HARCOURT. With many Illustrations.

THE DEVELOPMENT OF NAVIES DURING THE LAST HALF-CENTURY. By Captain EARDLEY WILMOT, R.N. With Illustrations and Plans.

UNIFORM WITH THE ABOVE.

THE WAR IN THE PENINSULA. By ALEXANDER INNES SHAND. With Four Portraits on Copper, and Six Plans. Cloth, 5s.

AFRICA IN THE NINETEENTH CENTURY. By EDGAR SANDERSON. With Four Portraits on Copper, and a Map. Cloth, 5s.

LONDON: SEELEY AND CO., LTD., 38 GREAT RUSSELL ST.

BY THE SAME AUTHOR.

ANIMALS AT WORK AND PLAY.
Their Activities and Emotions.
By C. J. CORNISH.

With Twelve Illustrations. Second Edition. Price 6s.

'Always entertaining and generally informing, he has indeed written a delightful book.'—*World.*

'How thoroughly Mr. Cornish is a master of his subject we need not say; he writes of that which he knows, and he writes very brightly.'—*Globe.*

'Mr. Cornish has a way of working curiously suggestive, and of setting forth such subjects as "The Animal in Captivity" from the animal's point of view solely. As a result, his book contains a very fascinating series of chapters.' *Graphic.*

'Such a book as Mr. Cornish's shows how much there is to repay the intelligent observer of Nature.'—*Times.*

'A collection of short, chatty, delightful papers.'—*Bookseller.*

'Good as the former books were, we are disposed to think that this is even better still.'—*Spectator.*

NIGHTS WITH AN OLD GUNNER
And other Studies of Wild Life.
By C. J. CORNISH.

With Sixteen Illustrations by LANCELOT SPEED, CHARLES WHYMPER, *and from Photographs. Price 6s.*

'A most delightful volume of essays on country life and sport and charming studies of wild life.'—*Spectator.*

'The Old Gunner is a very entertaining personage, and his wit and wisdom come freshly to jaded ears. This is the best thing Mr. Cornish has done. Mr. Speed's drawings merit special praise. His "Mist of Ducks" crossing the moon is magnificent.'—*Black and White.*

'Mr. Cornish has eyes to see and he uses them: he has the skill to describe that which he has seen easily, gracefully, and accurately.'—*Country Life.*

'Both instructive and entertaining, as ever must be the record of a careful and painstaking observer of wild life who wields a pen always bright and often brilliant.'—*Illustrated London News.*

LONDON: SEELEY AND CO., LTD., 38 GREAT RUSSELL ST.

BY THE SAME AUTHOR.

LIFE AT THE ZOO.
Notes and Traditions of the Regent's Park Gardens.

By C. J. CORNISH.

Illustrated by Photographs by GAMBIER BOLTON. *Fifth Edition.*
Crown 8vo. Price 6s.

'A more companionable book we cannot imagine.'—*Spectator.*

'An account of the habits and nature of the inmates of the lordly prison-house in the Regent's Park, and of some of their past or future companions. The book is of absorbing interest throughout.'—*Daily News.*

'A charming series of sketches that form a pleasant medley for the lover of animals. The illustrations form a welcome addition.'—*Saturday Review.*

'Every lover of animals will find abundance of attraction and entertainment in Mr. Cornish's delightful volume.'—*Times.*

WILD ENGLAND OF TO-DAY
And the Wild Life in it.

By C. J. CORNISH.

Illustrated by Drawings and Photographs. Second Edition.
Demy 8vo. Price 12s. 6d.

'Mr. Cornish has undoubtedly found his true vocation in describing his experiences of country scenery and animal life. We have seldom derived more enjoyment from the perusal of a book of its kind.'—*Athenæum.*

'Every chapter has the charm of wild life and of the fresh unsullied country.'—*Scotsman.*

'This work is even more fascinating than its predecessor. Everybody will find something to his taste in this choice volume of nature-lore.'—*World.*

'Those of us who are left in town in the dull days will seem, in reading these pages, to sniff the fresh sea breezes, to hear the cries of the sea-bird and the songs of the wood-bird, to be conscious of the murmuring stream and waving forests and all the wild life that is therein.'—*St. James's Gazette.*

LONDON: SEELEY AND CO., LTD., 38 GREAT RUSSELL ST.

www.ingramcontent.com/pod-product-compliance
Lightning Source LLC
Chambersburg PA
CBHW030742250426
43672CB00028B/348